Rugs and Carpets of Europe and the Western World

Rug from Greek Islands—Crete—about thirty years old, which was embroidered on the loom. *Collection of Marian Miller. Photo by Jeanne G. Weeks.*

Jeanne G. Weeks and Donald Treganowan

RUGS AND CARPETS

of Europe and the Western World

Chilton Book Company
Philadelphia New York London

The authors would like to express gratitude and thanks to the following people whose personal efforts have greatly helped to enrich these chapters: Kathleen Darby, London, England; Viscount Garnock, Director, John Crossley and Sons Ltd., Halifax, England; Mikko Immonen, formerly of the Finnish Embassy, New York City; and Armi Ratia, Helsinki, Finland.

Published in Philadelphia by Chilton Book Company
and simultaneously in Ontario, Canada,
by Thomas Nelson & Sons, Ltd.

Library of Congress Catalog Card Number 70-99605
Designed by Warren Infield
Manufactured in the United States of America by
Quinn & Boden Company, Inc., Rahway, N.J.

CONTENTS

INTRODUCTION

Arachne, the daughter of Idimion of Colophony, who lived on the coast of Lydia was very proud of her special craft—that of weaving beautiful tapestries and rugs. Her pride was such that one day she had the effrontery to challenge Minerva, goddess and protectress of the arts and crafts of weaving and embroidery. Her challenge was to prove once and for all that she, Arachne, could outdo the goddess in both dexterity of weaving as well as in the beauty of her designs and colors. Unfortunately, she did; for although the tapestry woven by Minerva was of great beauty and grace, that of Arachne was more beautiful. In a fit of rage Minerva lost all control, picked up her shuttle and struck Arachne. Not satisfied with this, she then changed the lovely but arrogant Arachne into a spider.

The foregoing myth appears in Ovid's *Metamorphoses*, giving it Greek origin. An earlier historian, writing the *History of Heaven*, attributed a similar story to the Egyptians, who on a number of monuments had carved the figure of a woman holding a distaff in her right hand and nearby the form of a spider. To Egyptians, those figures have come to represent the art of tapestry or rug weaving.

Although no one knows when the history of carpet and rug weaving did begin, the recent openings of a number of Middle Eastern burial sites have brought to light Oriental rugs of great beauty and clarity of color, which pre-date the first century by some five hundred years. One, an early Pazruk, was found in the East Turkestan site of Lou Lan, which dates back to that time. A much younger rug of exceptional beauty, a Sassanian rug, was found and called "Spring of Chosroes" (named after Chosroes I, who ruled Persia from 531 to 579 A.D.). But from very early times carpets have been a symbol of luxury woven for men of wealth and attainment.

During the eighth century the floor of the palace of the Baghdad of Harun-al-Rashid was covered with more than twenty-two thousand carpets. Many people working many hours were needed to weave that many carpets, for a vii fine Oriental carpet possesses about eight hundred hand-tied knots per square inch. A carpet measuring eleven by fifteen feet, knotted by a highly skilled and rapid craftsman, would still take almost eight to nine hundred days to finish and bind.

The word "carpet" is derived from the Latin word "carpere," meaning to pluck. It is possible the early word meant the plucking of wool from sheep, but more realistically the word could have come from the motion of hands in the act of tying each knot onto the warp thread. In any case, modern usage implies a rug of a large size—generally no less than eight by ten feet. Smaller ones are called rugs, and the very small ones, mats.

Whether carpet or rug, it should stand up under hard wear. Those textiles, although woven in the same manner as carpets or rugs, but which cannot stand up to hard wear, must be termed tapestries or table rugs. Within the category of carpets and rugs there are two classifications, those with smooth face and those with a pile. Within those general qualifications, over the years, there has been an abundance of beautiful designs and patterns reflecting many different cultural backgrounds.

Although this book concerns itself with carpets and rugs woven within the last five to six hundred years in Europe, Scandinavia, and America—the western or occidental world—the craft of weaving was perfected centuries earlier by sophisticated and creative peoples living in the so-called eastern or oriental world. Their designs, though limited to geometric forms and floral patterns, as dictated by religious dogma, were imaginative and exquisite. But without the knowledge and skill of those oriental craftsmen, weavers in the more primitive countries of the western world could never have excelled in creating the equally beautiful carpets and rugs of a totally different style and design about which we write.

There is a certain continuity within the history of rug and carpet weaving which starts with those ancient Sassanian weavers and continues throughout the Middle East, finally moving to the west with the Moorish craftsmen who moved into Spain. The fascinating problem is not that the French, British, and American weavers each learned from successive generations of craftsmen who followed in orderly historical manner those Moors who originally taught in Spain, but that people in such isolated territories as Finland and the southwestern United States should weave a tapestry stitch in the same manner and with designs that do have a link with some hidden past. The Scandinavian craftsmen undoubtedly learned the craft from Balkan nomads, who centuries before made a pilgrimage to those countries. The nomads wove kilims (flat-weave rugs) to cover the openings of their tents to keep out cold and rain, or wrapped their few possessions in them while moving from one secure place to the other. But the craft as discovered within the American Indian culture, which predated the conquest of Mexico by the Spanish, remains a mystery.

Introduction

Carpet and rug designs remained static in the various countries or areas, sometimes for many centuries at a time. Proof of this is most noticeable when a student can quickly identify a carpet (particularly an Oriental) and place it within its own region. The explanation is quite simple. Weavers were almost never creative artists. They were craftsmen who plied a trade with proficiency. It was the artist, or some other outside influence, who developed the initial design that then was copied and recopied, often with some slight variation or embellishment, by subsequent generations of weavers. Whereas the identity of the original artist has long faded into history, the finished carpet or rug remains a testament to the craftsman who wove it with great patience and care.

In modern times, the artist draws or paints a scale model for his carpet design. This is called a cartoon. Today's cartoons are generally scaled down to an inch representing a foot. A few artists, particularly those who work with the weavers of Aubusson, prefer instead to create a full scale painting rather than the traditional scaled down cartoon, thereby injecting a multitude of details which the craftsman at Aubusson recreates in wool with an almost unbelievable skill. In early times, unlimited copies were made from an original design, and long after the initial drawing or painting was destroyed, one carpet would serve as cartoon for the next. Present day cartoons are designed on an exclusive basis for the customer (often represented by an interior designer or architect), who prefers to own a one-of-a-kind carpet or rug. Some decorative rugs or carpets are made for showroom dealers on a limited-edition basis, and the design can, if needed, be rescaled or recolored.

1 SPAIN

A CURIOUS PASTICHE of both Christian and Moslem symbols and motifs pervades all of the early Spanish domestic designs. This peculiar blend of Eastern and Western decorative styles known as *mudejar* has set apart all of the early Spanish creative arts from those of other Western European countries.

Like England, France, and Italy, Spain was once a part of the great Roman Empire. It is difficult to tell just how people lived in Hispania (as the Iberian Peninsula was called at that time) under Roman rule, for few vestiges of any buildings have survived to indicate whether homes possessed either charm or comfort, or whether architecture in general reached any level of significance. For early in the fifth century A.D. a primitive army of warrior Christians, the Visigoths, swept down from the north and literally demolished all that had been built during the nearly five centuries of Roman life on that huge peninsula. Only fragmented traces of buildings which include the tiers of an amphitheatre at Sagunto and ruins of some buildings at Merido, were left.

Many of the patrician families of modern Spain trace their ancestry not to the Romans, but to these Christians who remained peacefully settled in

3

small communities in the plains and mountains until well into the eighth century A.D. Over the years, however, the warm climate of the fruitful valleys of Spain slowly sapped the virility of these northern warriors, and because of the small size and relative isolation of each of these small communities, all were easily dispersed in the eighth century when an invasion of Moslem Moors—religious zealots fighting in the name of Allah—drove these Christians far to the north of Spain.

The Visigoths were mainly farmers and traders; they were neither artists nor craftsmen. Weaving was limited to the simple task of making fabric for clothing. It seems strange, however, that many who were traders traveling to and from the exotic and dazzling world of North Africa and often to the city of Constantinople with its incredibly beautiful architecture, brilliant mosaics, and homes filled with fine furnishings, were not moved by some desire to recreate objects of beauty for their own pleasure at home. But once again after the invasion, this time by the Moors, nothing remains to indicate that life in these communities was other than primitive and un-sophisticated, for the few scattered ruins left standing indicate that buildings were both crude and austere.

Unlike the Visigoths, the Moors or Saracens ("People of the Desert")— a polyglot of Arabs, Syrians, Egyptians, and Berbers—were a sophisticated and educated people. Many of the final settlers were scholars, mystics, and poets. They came from a country which had attained a high level of civilization and personal luxury. Their domestic architecture was both complex and beautiful, with interiors rich with luxurious tapestries, Oriental carpets from Persia or Asia Minor, and furniture. Both the Moslem Moors, and their traditional neighbors, the North African Jews, were business men and world traders, and as such, many had amassed considerable wealth, setting standards of great personal sophistication in their homes, mosques, in educa-tion, and in their public life.

To make life agreeable in the strange primitive Spanish countryside, many Moors brought with them not only household treasures but craftsmen skilled in the arts of silk weaving, building, mosaic work, wood carving, and in the smithing of gold and silver (damascening). Palaces and villas were built throughout the central plains and southern highlands, and cities were established. Architecture and interior furnishings were unparalleled, with a splendor barely matched in Spain since. The city of Cordoba, the Islamic capitol of Spain established in 756 A.D., became second only to Constantinople in size and grace. The Moors called it their "Bride of

Andalusia." Within the heart of this great city, the fascinating mosque was started during the eighth century and finally completed during the eleventh century. It still stands as a tribute to the great artistry and extraordinary craftsmanship of the Moors. It was only many years later that the mosque was converted into a Christian sanctuary. Cordoba today is also known for its fine Moroccan tooled leather—an art developed from an early Moorish craft. These leathers were originally used both as mats on the floors and to cover chairs and chests. In later years, the latter were often studded with large nails. The Moors were also supreme artisans in metal work and in damascening, an art which has been passed down through the ages and establishments in the city of Toledo and these crafts are still carried on there.

The Golden Age of Spain can be dated from the second generation of virile young men, Spanish Moors, who lived side by side with the young Christian knights of the north, such as Berbardo del Carpio, with whom they fought against the Franks (French) at Roncevalles. Even El Cid, it is said, once took service with the Spanish Moor. This period of strength and elegance lasted through the Renaissance, ending with the reign of Philip II (grandson of Joan the Mad) who died in 1598. It was Philip who built the famous but gloomy Escoril palace.

The Moors, however, remained in full power within the country only until well into the ninth century A.D., when Charlemagne (Charles I of France), self-proclaimed king of the Christian Occident, drove them from many of their strongholds back over the Spanish Sierras into the province of Andalusia, where they remained until 1492. But the significant contributions left by these people remain an integral part of the life and culture of that piquant country today.

While the Moors were so industriously building the central and southern portions of the country, further north the Christian communities of Spaniards grew into a series of small, independent Medieval kingdoms: Navarre, Aragon, Castile, Catalonia—all familiar names today. Through respect and commerce with their Moorish neighbors, these small kingdoms developed into important provinces. Here were built the cities of Segovia, Madrid, Zaragosa, and others. During the early growth of these young cities and provinces the people naturally turned, not to their primitive neighbors to the north in France, but to these irresistible neighbors to the South, the Moors, for guidance and for matters of education. Emulation of a lavish and knowledgeable way of life unknown further north became chic, a result of uninhibited travel throughout the peninsula. The first Queen of Navarre, during a short trip to the south, made a personal visit to the reigning Caliph of Cordoba and was dazzled by her friendly reception and certainly no less by her surroundings. Rooms in the palace were lined with beautiful carpets, tapestries, and mosaics. Food was served on gold plates encrusted with jewels. The carpets, though Oriental in style, as were all carpets at that time, may well have been woven on Spanish soil, either in Chinchilla or Valencia, both cities within the Spanish province of Murcia. For the carpet industry established there during the early years of the Moorish settlement is believed to have been the first within the Islamic world independent of, but similar to, the early industries in Persia and Asia Minor. Hispano-Moresque rugs from this province are known to have been sold in markets in Egypt well into the fifteenth century, at which time an independent industry of its own was established in Cairo.

The spirit of co-existence in Spain between Christians and Moors lasted until the mid-fifteenth century, at which time two of the larger northern kingdoms were united through the marriage of Ferdinand II of Aragon and Isabella of Castile—both Christian zealots. Together they amassed a formidable army which, in a few years time, pushed the Moors back over the southern mountains of Spain and ultimately back across the sea to Africa, thereby creating a unified country once again under a single religious banner. The year 1492 not only marked the historic voyage of Christopher Columbus, but the Christian unification of Spain and the beginning of one of the most violent eras of despotism known to mankind, the Inquisition. Asylum was granted by the court, however, to a number of the fine Moorish craftsmen who had contributed so much to the splendor of the Moorish and Spanish courts. Included within this group of talented Moors were the famous weavers of carpets.

The Baronial Carpets of Spain

The light of Spain brilliantly points up the many colors of the countryside which range from the soft grays of olive trees to the deep red of the clay underneath. Shadows made by clouds in azure skies cast mauve and purple shades across the hillsides. In other sections there are pale yellow, dusty, arid plains, extremely hot in summer and, under driving winds, bitter cold in the winter. Spanish architecture, known for its quiet inner courtyards and cloisters with small interior gardens, was designed not only for privacy but as a protection against the weather. The ground floors in homes were, and still are, paved with tiles, stones, or brick, partially for coolness in summer, and partially against insects. On upper levels, where the family lived during the cold winter months, wood was used on the floor. The tiles were devoid of patterns and were generally a terra-cotta color, the color of the baked red clay. Bricks were often laid in herringbone patterns. In baronial homes, thick carpets covered areas of the floor while less fortunate families used interestingly woven heavy grass matting. In early days, cordovan leather mats were sometimes placed in front of chairs. A traditional fine linen matting is still being made on the Island of Majorca. It has a lengua (tongue) pattern, a form of zig-zag taken from a similar Moorish design.

But the early baronial carpets woven in Spain were made of wool. The warp was generally white, although red or yellow warps have been seen. The Hispano-Moresque (carpets of Oriental design made within Spain), and later the *mudejar* (carpets of combined Islamic and Christian design motifs made in Spain), usually incorporated a scheme of elementary colors: red, blue, green, yellow, and white. Occasionally black and white carpets did appear. These have been referred to as mourning carpets, to be placed on the coffin before burial. There is no evidence or document to verify this fact, but it is highly possible that a few did exist, in which case the date and coat of arms, were woven into this pattern. Red was the official color of the city of Granada, which the Moors called their "City of Dawn." Green and white were known as colors of good fortune. Also popular were blue and yellow in varying shades.

The most important early styles in Spain were the heraldic carpets known as Admiral carpets (the earliest of these were woven for families and descendants of Spanish admirals, a rank of considerable status). These were long, narrow carpets embellished with coats of arms and ornamented with such devices as shields in the center of the field and bordered with thin Kufic (Persian) script. Often the coat of arms was displayed in compartmented form or in corners. The long, narrow shape of the carpet during these early times is unique and sometimes a factor in identifying age. The narrowness has been attributed to the narrow looms found in convents, but actually baronial houses of the times had many long narrow corridors leading from one main reception room to another, and these long narrow carpets were used to enhance the vista.

One of the most important Moorish symbols was the pomegranate; this appears in many Spanish textiles—silks and tapestries as well as carpets. Inscriptions were used as ornament, sometimes as an overall ground pattern. These were Kufic (Persian) or Coptic (Egyptian) calligraphic inscriptions which sometimes related ancedotes or tales of exploits of the person for whom the carpet was being woven. In this case they appeared as a large pattern filling the central ground, or these scripts were worked into border patterns. Often they were used for purely decorative purposes or entwined with other ornaments. By degrees, these inscriptions became pure ornament as angular ribbon-work, and still later as floral devices or sparce, leafy vines. When Spanish carpets have animal or human figures in the pattern they most certainly are the embodiment of the *mudejar* period, for the Islamic Koran, or sacred book, absolutely forbids the use of these forms for decorative purposes, calling this a form of idolatry. Large round wreath patterns in repeat or as large central medallions closely follow earlier oriental designs. Some symbols are star forms derived from the Seal of Solomon and the Star of David. The sacred tree—often referred to as the "tree of life" and adopted into many Western cultures—also appears in Spanish carpet designs.

With the exception of the peasant rugs woven on the slopes of the southern Alpujarra mountains, the carpet industry was located mainly in the east central areas of Spain—close to the meadows and rivers where sheep were raised. The earliest known center in Western Europe, Chinchilla, appears to have been inhabited before the Romans by Copt artisans (early Christian settlers from Egypt), about whom, it has been said but not documented, that many were weavers. But by the late fourteenth and fifteenth centuries a recognized and active industry was located at Letur, where the early so-called "Admiral" carpets were woven. Here also were carpets with small geometric patterns. Many of these carpets were huge in size, although no one can tell just how large, for over the years almost all have been chopped up. Those still in existence are in fragments. A few have been found patched together, but these still give us only a very sketchy idea of the original size.

By the sixteenth and early seventeenth century, the industry moved to Alcaraz. Here, too, baronial carpets of exceptional size were woven. Patterns shifted. The so-called artichoke pattern was developed here. Indigenous to this region were the wreath pattern, the dragon or phoenix borders (sometimes called snakes) and animals, or animal forms in borders.

All carpets woven both in Letur and Alcaraz were woven with the single knot (so-called Spanish knot), developed in an effort to emulate the crisp pattern definitions of the famous Spanish silk weaves, the finest in the world at that time. Many of the carpet patterns were actually adaptations of silk designs.

Later, the industry moved to the north, to Cuenca, during the seventeenth and eighteenth centuries. Here carpets were easier to identify, for the weave reverted once again to the more coarse and stout double loop or Ghiordes knot weave. Dyes were not as clear as those of Letur and Alcaraz.

The Royal Manufactory of Madrid was established under the patronage of Philip V (1683–1746). It was headed by a weaver of Flemish origin, Miguel Stuyck, who wove rugs and carpets in the French Savonnerie style and manner. The center still exists under the direction of Stuyck's descendants. During the 19th and 20th centuries, the Royal Manufactory of Madrid reproduced many fine French Savonnerie designs, woven with such finesse that today's collector finds it difficult to identify them from originals.

It must be noted that although the carpet weaving industry moved to new locations over the years, a few weavers always remained behind in the older locations, continuing to weave and to teach the local craftsmen the arts of rug weaving. By the nineteenth century, carpets still emanated from all of these traditional weaving centers.

The Gothic era (1492–1516) and the early Renaissance through the reign of Philip II were known as the Golden Age of Spanish culture. Much of the furniture being reproduced today and called Spanish or Colonial Spanish (in Mexico and South America), architectural woodwork such as the great carved doors, and most of the fine silk patterns date from this period. Court dresses and ceremonial robes were lavish.

After the banishment of the Moors from Spain by Ferdinand and Isabella, trade with the Christian countries of France and Italy was expanded. Noble families within all three countries intermarried, and through these liaisons new textile patterns, such as the French fleur-de-lys, became incorporated into Spanish coats of arms. From Italy came such Italian Renaissance symbols as cornucopias, vases, garlands, allegorical animals, and the ubiquitous acanthus leaf, symbol of classic Rome.

The last of the Moorish craftsmen who remained under asylum were finally expelled from Spain in 1609, and from that time on there was a distinct downward trend in the quality of the crafts within the country. The city born Spaniard had little inclination to adapt himself to the crafts and specifically to that of the complicated art of carpet weaving. As the Spaniard seemed incapable of any creative imagination, many of the domestic crafts reverted to copies of their earlier designs, and carpets to the Oriental styles unfortunately of an infinitely inferior quality.

Alpujarras—the Peasant Rugs of Spain

Nestled among the Alpujarra mountains in the Province of Granada is one of the most fertile valleys in the world. The hillsides abound with rushing brooks and streams. The word Alpujarra means "grasslands," and the countryside is in dramatic contrast to the heat-cracked plains of central Spain. There are numerous towns dotting the area, and long before Columbus discovered America, one such town, Jaen, was noted for its beautiful fabrics. That Moorish craftsmen settled in the area appears certain. It is easier, however, to identify the peasant rugs and carpets from this region—now in private collections—for they are dated in the corner, with many bearing names or initials of the people who were to receive them. These carpets, also woven on narrow looms, were originally woven as covers for the marriage bed (mantas) and for canvas-topped carriages (to keep out the heat). Larger carpets or rugs were made up of two or three "bedspreads" sewn together. Often large, fancifully knotted fringes, sometimes as long as eight to ten inches, were sewn around the rug, making them somewhat impractical for the floor. These fringes were in solid colors, a color usually taken from the central pattern. The rugs had a rough texture formed by raised loops of wool.

The weaving technique was quite different from the one or two thread pile weaves of the Hispano-Moresque or *mudejar* carpets discussed earlier. These rugs were coarse and thick and were quite heavy, in keeping with the rugged personality of the surrounding mountains. These were made on looms with a weft, or filler, thread looped over the warp threads. A stiff iron rod was used to wind the weft thread into loops. When one row of loops was wound they were then woven into the warp, which was then enmeshed tightly into the fabric of the carpet by a beater. This process was generally repeated until five rods were tightly woven into the warp. Then the first rod was pulled out to become number six, and so forth until the rug was completed. The coarseness of these rugs was also attributed to the thickness of the spun wool.

The designs were unsophisticated, often very personal, their inspiration taken directly from nature. Frequently a tree-of-life pattern appeared with large birds. These were drawn with no thought to scale, the bird appearing a good deal larger than the tree, for instance. Sometimes vases, with or without flowers, borders of grapes and vines, stars, rearing lions, and pomegranates, the symbol of Granada, were used. These appeared in as many as six colors, but two were more likely: blue, off-white, red, black; red and green; or combinations of red, blue, white, honey yellow, or clear yellow were also favorites.

After the Moors left Spain the peasants of the Alpujarra region continued to weave their rugs for marriage chests or other personal reasons. The cross and chalice, both Christian symbols began to appear in designs. The double-headed eagle of Charles V and occasionally a coat of arms, complete with names and sometimes addresses, were also woven into the central field or in corners.

The Alpujarra rug woven today, popular with interior designers because of bright colors and the refreshingly naive patterns, has been refined, slightly restyled, and recolored for the contemporary home. But it still retains all of the distinctive charm of the early Alpujarra rugs of the eighteenth and nineteenth centuries.

Spanish, Mudejar, mainly Spanish
knot. Middle XV century. Fragment
of two systems of design, possibly
from Letur, it was once a common
design but is rare now. *The Textile
Museum, Washington, D. C.*

Spanish, circa 1470–80, probably Alcaraz. *The Metropolitan Museum of
Art, Cloisters Fund, 1961.*

14

Spanish, Mudejar, Spanish knot. 1st half XV century. Letur or Alcaraz. Runner with three squares, star pattern. *The Textile Museum, Washington, D. C.*

Spanish, Mudejar, single knot. Fragment, XV century. Alcaraz wool pile and warp, cotton weft. Medallion pattern, part of border on each side of a rose field. *The Textile Museum, Washington, D. C.*

Spanish, Cuenca (?), Spanish knot. Renaissance. XV century. "Wreath Carpet" with a fragment garland and border of many shades of blue on a coral ground. Segment of a second garland. *The Textile Museum, Washington, D. C.*

Spanish, wool, XV century. *The Metropolitan Museum of Art, Rogers Fund, 1913.*

16

Spanish, Hispano-Moresque. XV century. Detail of an "Admiral" carpet. *The Metropolitan Museum of Art, Bequest of George Blumenthal, 1941.*

Spanish, Hispano-Moresque. XV century. Arms of Maria of Castille, Queen of Aragon. *Courtesy of the Hispanic Society of America.*

Spanish, Mudejar, Spanish loop. 2nd half XV century, Alcaraz. Gothic patterned rug. *The Textile Museum Washington, D. C.*

Spanish, Alcaraz (?), Spanish knot, single knot pile. Late XV century or early XVI. So-called Holbein octagons and arabesques. Taken from an Anatolian arabesque rug design, blue on yellow. *The Textile Museum, Washington, D. C.*

Spanish, wool. XV–XVI century. Armorial carpet. *The Metropolitan Museum of Art, George Blumenthal Bequest, 1941.*

Spanish, Mudejar, Spanish knot-wool, 1500.
Guadalajara runner. Four squares with octagonal
pattern. *The Textile Museum, Washington,
D. C.*

Spanish, Mudejar, Alcaraz. Stylized Spanish knot,
single knot pile. Late XV century. Cross of
Calatrava spears and lozenge grating, ducks in
border. *The Textile Museum, Washington, D. C.*

Top: Spanish, wool, 1500–1550. *The Metropolitan Museum of Art, Rogers Fund, 1913.*

Spanish, pile carpet section. Mid-XVI century. *The Art Institute of Chicago, Charles Deering Collection.*

Opposite, top: Spanish, Renaissance, Castille. Spanish knot, single knot. Wool weft and pile, cotton loop. Early XVI century. Possibly a tomb cover. "Exmemet Renascor" ("from myself I am reborn"). "Victoria Doctis" ("victory to the learned"). Phoenix rising from the flames in the middle of central medallion. Skull and cross bones in the corner medallions. *The Textile Museum, Washington, D. C.*

Opposite, below: Spanish, Alcaraz, single knot, Renaissance pattern. Second half XVI century. Yellow field, blue design. *The Textile Museum, Washington, D. C.*

Spanish, embroidered carpet, XVI century. *The Metropolitan Museum of Art, Rogers Fund, 1908.*

22

Spanish, wool. XVI century. *The Metropolitan Museum of Art, Rogers Fund, 1908.*

Spanish, XVI century. *Courtesy of The Hispanic Society of America.*

Opposite page:

Top, left: Spanish, Late XVI century. Arms of Dominican Order in corners. *Courtesy of The Hispanic Society of America.*

Top, right: Spanish, Mudejar. Spanish knot wool pile cotton loop and weft. Probably early XVII century. Fragment of a wreath pattern with a rose field; two borders remain with the main one in lighter blue. *The Textile Museum, Washington, D. C.*

Bottom, left: Spanish, linen and wool. XVII century. *The Metropolitan Museum of Art, Gift of James F. Ballard, 1922.*

Bottom, right: Spanish, XVII century. Embroidered with herringbone stitch. Embroidery inspired by a Persian medallion rug; three-lobed medallions are in a field with many identical or repeat details. Octagons in border. *The Textile Museum, Washington, D. C.*

This page:

Top: Spanish, XVIII century. Armorial or Admiral carpet. *Courtesy of Parke-Bernet Galleries, Berberyan Collection.*

Right: Spanish, XVIII century. *Courtesy of The Art Institute of Chicago.*

Spanish, XIX century. Cotton and wool. *Courtesy of The Art Institute of Chicago.*

Spanish, possibly an Alpujarra linen
on linen embroidery, 1550–1600. *The
Metropolitan Museum of Art, Rogers Fund, 1908.*

Spanish, possibly an Alpujarra,
wool. XVI century. *The Metropolitan Museum of Art, Rogers
Fund, 1908.*

Spanish, possibly an Alpujarra, wool and linen. Late XVIII century. *The Metropolitan Museum of Art, Gift of James M. Shoemaker, 1926.*

Spanish, Alpujarra. Welt loop wool pile resembles a hook rug. XIX century. Rose medallion center on blue ground, single border. Plants and animals. *The Textile Museum, Washington, D. C.*

Above, left: Spanish, possibly an Alpujarra, cotton and wool embroidery. XVIII century. *The Metropolitan Museum of Art, Rogers Fund Purchase, 1911.*

Above, right: Spanish, Alpujarra, Grenada province. Signed by Ana Segura, dated 1766. *Courtesy of The Hispanic Society of America.*

Spanish, Alpujarra, welt loop pile. Early XIX century. Plants and animals. *The Textile Museum, Washington, D. C.*

Opposite page: Spanish Alpujarra. *The Textile Museum, Washington, D. C.*

Spanish, Alpujarra. *The Textile Museum, Washington, D. C.*

Spanish, Alpujarra. *The Textile Museum, Washington, D. C.*

Spanish, Alpujarra. *The Textile Museum, Washington, D. C.*

Spanish, folk carpet of Bessarabian style. *Courtesy of Parke-Bernet Galleries, Berberyan Collection.*

2 FRANCE

Unlike the strong, forceful decorative styles of Spain—
a fusion of two dominant cultures, Christian and Islamic—French styles were
delightfully capricious. For, like fashion, they evolved from the whims and
personal tastes of kings, ladies of the court, and on occasion, prime ministers.
But in spite of this seemingly frivolous attitude, no country has supported the
artists and craftsmen who created its beautiful objets d'art, tapestries, and
carpets as has France. For beginning with the thirteenth century, the finest
artists and craftsmen of the country were pressed into the service of the
crown, and still later, were further protected by royal laws and edicts—these
to curb competition from imports and to maintain high quality standards.

The history of rugs and carpets in France starts, as far as the earliest
known documents can tell us, during the reign of Louis IX (1226–1270). It
was the time of the Holy War of The Crusaders. Louis IX was the leader
of the Christian army and much of his rule was spent on the battlefield.
Curiously enough, his adversary was the Moor, a descendant of the same
group which had settled several centuries earlier in Spain. Over the years
these people, escaping harassment, had trudged through the Pyrenees mountain passes from Spain into the southern regions of France.

35

In time, Louis was successful in ridding the country of these strange unchristian peoples, and as booty for the royal treasury he brought back an abundance of gold ornaments, jewels, and a large number of luxurious carpets. At the time the value of the carpets must have seemed secondary to the warm comfort they undoubtedly offered him during the cool nights on the battlefield. Like most of the carpets found in Spain during this period, these were Oriental in design. Many were apparently of Saracenic origin (the French referred to them as "Sarrasinian") but it has been speculated that a few of these captured carpets might have been woven on French soil by Moors, or even French craftsmen under Moorish guidance. What is certain, however, is that prior to the mid-thirteenth century, tapestries had been woven under Moorish influence in the village of Aubusson, in the Creuse region of France. The construction of those tapestries closely resembled that of the Oriental carpet; they were thick and woolly, not unlike present day Moroccan rugs.

The war in France lessened in 1254, and during the period which followed, there was a great deal of artistic creativity and construction. It was the Gothic age, a time when men's thoughts and energies were devoted to religion and to building great monuments. The Gothic cathedral became a symbol of the pious man's spiritual attachment to heaven.

In Paris, the King was developing a taste for simple luxury. For it was also a time when amenities of the sophisticated social life of Spain and Italy began to make an appearance at the French court. Entertainment became organized with a decorum fitting the religious tempo of the time. Musicals were held in the evening after dinner, as were poetry readings and small theatricals. Still later, hunting became fashionable, and during the latter half of the thirteenth century, royalty and the wealthy bourgeois built the first of the imposing hunting lodges and châteaux outside of Paris in which to idle away leisure hours. By the end of the fourteenth century the gay life had become irresistible, to the point where, at times, expenditure exceeded that of income. Happily though, France and the tourist today are the inheritors of over five centuries of the tremendous building program begun by these Gothic men.

The craftsmen pressed into action at this time were native Frenchmen, many of them Huguenots (Protestants). For unlike the Spaniard, the French were by nature artistic and creative.

Design was eclectic, for France had as yet to develop a domestic style of its own, either in architecture or in the decorative arts. Those early châteaux, or château-forts as they were called, though not exactly crude, were dark and cold, built to double as bastions against not infrequent skirmishes, some religious, and some from predatory neighbors. It was not until the fifteenth century, after the death of Joan of Arc—a time which coincided with the decline of the Gothic religious fervor—that France entered a period of artistic development identifiable with the French spirit. Italy was then in the heyday of the Renaissance, and the French viewed the luxury and beauty of her buildings, her paintings, and furnishings with some envy. Although France's neighbor to the south, Spain, had also developed an artistic force, it was to Italy with its more romantic style compatible with the French personality, that the designers of France looked for inspiration.

By the end of the fifteenth century, Louis XII (1498–1515) had brought to court a number of Italian artisans trained in the domestic arts and crafts, both to work and to train French craftsmen. His cousin, Francis I (1515–1547), continued the tradition, and by 1516 such luminaries as Leonardo da Vinci, followed in 1537 by the architect, Vignola, the muralist, Primaticcio, and the painter, Andrea del Sarto, were working for the French royal household. Thus the reign of Francis I historically marks the awakening of French domestic arts.

To the more sensitive eye of the Italian designers, French artisans were crude, lacking in finesse and delicacy, and in consequence hordes of Italian artisans were imported to teach and work. But in spite of the magnitude of this imported force, the amount of building was such that France enjoyed great economic gains. This was the era which saw the building of many of the fine châteaux of the Loire Valley, of the ever popular and beautiful Fontainebleau, and Blois, the favorite of Francis I. Blois, contrary to the delicate and feminine Italianate Fontainebleau, was masculine, huge and dark. The interior walls were painted with French coats of arms, surrounded by arabesques and mythical animal forms (both Italian motifs). In many other châteaux, walls were covered with Cordovan leather, or hung with tapestries. Where wood was used, it was carved with Gothic linenfold patterns—a motif often repeated on chairs, chests, and armories. Floors were covered with decorative tiles or paved with handsome parquetry in many patterns. At Blois, however, the private chambers of Francis I were lined with Vitruvian inlay patterns of Italian arabesques and candelabra forms. Into these decorations the letter F was entwined, as was the form of a salamander, an animal to which myth ascribes the power to withstand flame. This was the personal symbol within the French coat of arms used by Francis I.

At Fontainebleau the private rooms were entirely Italian in decoration. Aubusson tapestries hung on walls for warmth and, it is said, for acoustics. For by now the weavers at Aubusson were busily creating beautiful tapestries in the Arras manner (the French version of the Flemish weave), but as far as anyone can judge, no carpets were being woven in this distinguished center at this time.

Admiration for and emulation of Italian styles continued for five generations. Henry II (1547–1559), son of Francis I, and later Henry IV (1589–1610) (no blood relative whatsoever), continued to strengthen the social and political ties between the two countries by marrying Italian women.

The wife of Henry II, Catherine de Medici, a woman of great force which at times verged on despotism, brought a certain elegance to the French court, and by her natural good taste introduced all that was best of the Italian Renaissance tradition. As an intellectual, Catherine, Queen of France, created one of the most brilliant courts of the time, one which was to last long after the death of her frequently faithless husband. Henry, on the other hand, chose to occupy his own time expanding the elaborate building programs started by his father.

Henry's marriage to Catherine was somewhat of a personal burden. Among the many mistresses he enjoyed, one in particular, Diane de Poitiers, was the favorite. Much of the royal attentions were spent in establishing a second *menage*. The famous Château de Chenonceaux in the Loire Valley, and a Château d' Anet (where Diane de Poitiers was buried), were built with money of the crown as gifts to the beautiful Diane. It was at Anet that she preferred to live and where she maintained a splendid court. The building's decorative style was steeped in the prevailing Italian tradition, with ceilings and walls painted with Renaissance arabesques or marbleizing, or covered with domino papers. Within the private chambers set aside for Henry II, the barely discernible initials "H" and "D" were entwined among the curlicues of the elaborately painted ceiling and wall decorations. This was a petty deceit, considering the elaborate social life the two spent together within the walls and gardens of Anet. Within the château compound was an aviary of rare birds, a menagerie of leopards kept in readiness for the hunt, and a magnificent library.

It was, however, the artisans of France who were the ultimate beneficiaries of these building campaigns. For as more and more craftsmen were trained and pressed into service, they came under the personal supervision of the King and his architects. This was particularly true of those tapestry weavers at Aubusson (the forerunners of the famous carpet weavers at Aubusson), and in two newly established weaving centers, Tours and Felletin. Here, weavers were also trained in the very refined Arras tapestry weave, but the few carpets woven in these centers remained Oriental in character.

When Henry III (1574–1589) assumed his father's crown, he left many of the state and social problems to his mother. The country was once again embroiled in a series of religious wars, sharpened by the influx of Spanish Protestants fleeing the inquisition in Spain. Virtually all building stopped; the frivolities of social life were considered bad taste. Work at all craft centers, and in particular the weaving centers—outposts of Protestantism—came to a standstill. There was much strife and grief in the name of religion, which lasted well after the death of Henry III.

By contrast, the reign of Henry IV (1589–1610) was one of tolerance and creativity. The development of the carpet industry of France owes much to this Huguenot, born Prince of Navarre (a small kingdom in the Pyrenees near the Spanish border). In the name of religious freedom, Henry became leader of the forces opposing the Catholic Henry II and Catherine de Medici. Henry's success in the field had brought the battle to the gates of Paris, the last outpost of the Holy See. But the fiercely loyal citizens frantically rallied their forces to protect the court and church from the Huguenot. Henry of Navarre, a determined and wily man, amazed at the violence of the defense, and realizing he could lose the battle at the last bastion, resorted to a rather unusual tactic. He reversed his role in the ideological struggle. He became a Catholic. He has often been reported as having muttered as he did so, ". . . Paris is worth a mass." The people of Paris, admittedly baffled by this chameleon-like tactic, did open their gates, and finally, in 1593, crowned Henry of Navarre King Henry IV of all France.

At heart Henry remained loyal to the Huguenots and in 1593, as protection for all Protestants, including many of the fine craftsmen of the country, he issued the Edict of Nantes, allowing his friends complete freedom of worship. As a further act of generosity and to protect the famous weaving centers, Henry IV set down a further decree banning all importation of carpets and tapestries into the country. He also established, under his personal guidance, a weaving center within the huge complex of the Louvre, where carpets and tapestries were hand woven to resemble the Flemish style.

Later, in 1620, a second decree became necessary to confirm the rights of out-of-town French weavers to sell their carpets and tapestries within the city of Paris without paying the established tax or surcharge. Under his rule, protection was extended to include all types of artists and craftsmen within the country.

Henry IV married Marie de Medici and together they established a brilliant court, gathering around them the creative minds of the country. Once again the full resource of the crown was lavished on the furnishings for the many buildings acquired. The king's favorite château, Pau, was filled with sumptuous furnishings, including a number of important tapestries. Carpets for floors were only beginning to be considered a necessary part of the interior scheme but these still remained copies of Oriental styles. For weavers within the numerous and expanding carpet weaving establishments, though highly skilled craftsmen, were not artists. Instead, they copied with incredible finesse any design presented. As the creative artist was pursuing other areas of self expression, no new ideas or designs for carpets or rugs were forthcoming. Therefore Oriental carpet designs were copied and recopied. This state of affairs remained predominant until the end of the seventeenth century.

Of the reign of Henry IV, Voltaire (1776) once wrote

. . . although Henry IV may have been a great man, his era was not great in any way . . . the arts of peace, which form the charm of society, which beautifies cities, which illuminates the mind, which civilizes manners, all these began only in the age in which Louis XIV was born and died.

Life in France remained relatively stable throughout the reign of Henry IV and through that of his successor, Louis XIII (1610–1643). The decorative arts were still eclectic in style, although the number of important buildings increased.

In 1635, during the reign of Louis XIII, the Académie Française was established under the guidance of Cardinal de Richelieu, a self-proclaimed protector of society. The act of the Académie was to dignify the letters of France and to establish a codified dictionary of the French language. (This was completed in 1694.) But the formation of the Académie coincided with a wave of nationalism, which in turn filtered down through the various levels of society. Decorative furnishings at last began to come into focus, with a style indigenous to the French character—no longer influenced by Italy, Spain or the Flemish artists and weavers. The awakening was slow and only reached full fruition at the time of the son of Louis XIII, Louis XIV.

The reign of Louis XIV (1643–1715), "Le Roi Soliel," heralded the

French Renaissance. (A more definitive term for the arts of the period was "Baroque.") It was an age of specialization. Architects designed and built the great buildings, interior decorators embellished them with lavish furnishings in complete harmony with the exterior and interior architecture. Silks, tapestries, and carpets were woven by the most skilled of trained weavers; furniture was designed and carved by great ebonists. The style, developed from the supreme classical architectural proportions of Imperial Rome, was monumental and somewhat masculine in feeling. This was no happenstance; it was carefully planned. The mastermind was Colbert, the dynamic Minister of Finance, who after the death of Richelieu became chief advisor to Louis XIV. (It can be said that Colbert was the image builder for his king.) All buildings, furnishings, and the pomp surrounding the king were designed with one purpose in mind: the glorification of the king, the crown, the state.

Under the guise of paternalism, Colbert encouraged improvements in the textile, carpet, and tapestry weaving centers in order to hire and train more craftsmen to produce the elaborate silks, carpets and tapestries needed.

Colbert himself went to Flanders in search of artists who could create designs specifically suited to both tapestry and carpets for court use. The duty of these artists, once established on French soil, was to teach both weavers and apprentices methods of dying wool and design, all calculated to improve the existing standards of performance. The title of apprentice became more difficult to obtain. Training was arduous and long, but because of this imposed control, the final products of their work did become, and remain today, the finest in the world.

As a result of the court's activity, there was an upsurge in the general economy and an attendant national stability. Great architectural talents were engaged. Included was Louis Le Vau who, in 1657, built one of the most beautiful châteaux in the world, Vaux-le-Vicomte near Melun. (This was for Fouquet, Superintendent of Finance before he fell out of favor at court, was arrested, and finally imprisoned. Molière, LaFontaine, and Jean Baptiste Lully were part of the Fouquet intellectual galaxy which inhabited Vaux-le-Vicomte.) The famous architect, François Mansart and later his nephew, Jules Hardouin-Mansart, were also chosen as court architects, as was the landscape artist, André Le Nôtre, and the artist and interior decorator, Charles LeBrun (LeBrun painted the murals at Versailles and the ceiling frescoes in the Apollo room at the Louvre). LeBrun was the court's favorite artist. It was he who set up an absolute dictatorship over all interior decorations from floor plan to chair covering, from door handle to carpet, or ceramic. He created a homogeneity of style, one in complete harmony with the spirit of Roman dignity, but also one truly French. The most dazzling and monumental work of the LeVau-LeBrun-Le Nôtre team was, of course, the expansion of a small hunting lodge originally built by Louis XIII, called Versailles. (Later, wings were added by the young Jules Hardouin-Mansart.) Under the guidance of Colbert the buildings were planned, and the gardens laid out in the impressive, artistic, and dignified manner we see today. The extensions of the Louvre Palace, many hunting lodges, and châteaux were also built.

For privacy from the hordes of people—guests, writers, musicians, ladies-in-waiting, young nobles, servants, to say nothing of mistresses—all housed in the greatly enlarged Versailles (which could, and finally did house 10,000 people), Louis XIV built for himself the Grand Trianon.

The Baroque Period was noted for its impressive court carpets, by now considered an important and integral part of the interior setting. The decorative style was basically classic, with line and proportion exquisitely balanced. Elaborate scrolls, acanthus leaves, insignia, cartouches, emblems of royalty, trophies, and a few flowers dominated the central areas of the impressive Savonnerie and Aubusson carpets. Borders were relatively simple, repeating the acanthus motifs, or faceted jewel patterns. Corners were "crossed" with fleurs-de-lys, or more acanthus leaves. Crossed or twisted ribbons (*gillochis*) often appeared. Color was brilliant, but used in a restrained manner, with fields of blue, tan, black, soft green, or muted red.

In the declining years of Louis XIV, Madame de Maintenon, a devoutly religious Catholic (who started her life in court as governess for the children, later became mistress, and still later, wife), held considerable influence over her husband the King. Under her direction, and in a weak moment, Louis XIV made one of the few great mistakes in judgment for France. In 1685 he revoked the Edict of Nantes. At a time when French decorative crafts had reached a true art form, many of the craftsmen were forced to leave the country, some going to the weaving centers in Flanders, others to Holland or America. It has been estimated that some sixty thousand fled to England.

Following the death of Louis XIV, a regency (1715–1723) was set up to handle the affairs of state. The young great grandson and successor to the throne was still a child of five. The Regence was a collective government facing a reactionary country, tired of the religious morality imposed upon it, and tired of a near disastrous inflation. The Regence maintained only a tempering influence over the rich nobility which, suffering its own reaction, had set up a new society of elegance and refinement.

The heritage of Louis XIV, however, was peace. But the period of "teaching the rich how to live" was over. Nobles and rich middle class, under the economic tensions of the period, began to take a more personal interest in their own decorating. The evolving style was charming, and modest by comparison with the grandiose Baroque style just finished. It was during this period that the simpler country style known today as French Provincial came into being. This style was more in keeping with the scale of the newer country manors dictated by a tightened budget.

Court styles were in transition, somewhere between two strong opposing forces: the impersonal Baroque design dictated by the Colbert clique, and the more intimate Romantic Rococo style of Louis XV. The Regence incorporated a little of both. Naturalism and symmetry were absolute. Two foreign influences added some confusion. From Italy, the studied symbols of the popular stylized Comedia dell'Arte (masks, grotesques, fantastic figures and forms), and from the Far East, chinoiserie with singerie (mischievous monkeys) and winged dragons. The classic coquille (shell) with its symmetrical fan of flutings made its appearance as a particularly dominant motif. (This was to last in various forms for many centuries.)

When Louis XV (1723–1774) came into power he had no thought of enhancing himself with great acts by which he might be immortalized. He wanted to enjoy life in intimacy and in luxury. His was a life of self-indulgence, disastrous to the country, and his well touted words, "Après moi, le déluge," were prophetic.

Louis XV was a restless man, difficult to amuse. He tired easily of his pleasures and was always bored. Madame de Pompadour, his favorite, one day described her triumphal career as mistress by saying, "Pity me, but do not blame me." The poor lady was hard pressed to invent new and original distractions and amusements. Amateur theatricals and little supper parties were meant to create a pleasing contrast to the pomp and more formal state affairs at the court of Versailles. She undertook the construction and decorating of country pleasure houses, such as the Ermitage at Fontainebleau, where the King could spend relaxed and intimate hours in the company of a few well chosen companions—all, of course, devoted to the mistress. In the little over twenty years in favor, she built, bought, rented, decorated, or redecorated with finesse and exquisite taste the Hôtel d'Évreux in Paris (today the Élysée Palace, home of the President of the Republic), Château de Bellevue, Château de Ménars (Loire), Château d'Auvilliers (Normandy), Château de Crécy near Dreux, summer houses of LaCelle, Montretout, and

Bimborion, and lastly the Ermitage close to the principle royal palaces at Compiègne and Fontainebleau. From time to time she sold these to the King (who had originally financed them) when she needed money for her debts. When Madame de Pompadour died in 1764, she left what remained of her possessions to her brother the Marquis de Marigny (appointed Chargée d'Affaires of all the King's buildings). He divided most of the property between Louis XV and her best friends.

The style known as Rococo was relatively informal. Everything was contrived to create intimacy and coziness. The large formal rooms at both the Louvre and Versailles were divided up and made into smaller spaces. Furniture was scaled down. The common denominator of design was a capricious love of curved, irregular, and asymmetrical lines, whether appearing in boiserie on the walls, in furniture, or in textiles. The style was in revolt against the rigid and intellectually balanced classic forms of the Baroque.

Patronage of the crafts was not through the crown as heretofore, but at the whim of ladies of the court who dictated their own style. This was a romantic time, as illustrated by naturalistic patterns. Carpets, silks, and boiserie were embellished with country flowers spilling out of baskets, ladies' sunbonnets, or in delightful bunches tied with ribbons. As much as Madame de Pompadour loved the role of social arbitor, Madame duBarry, her contender for the affections of the King, loved the pastoral pleasures of the countryside. Symbols of love and femininity abounded—the coquille, the lyre, crossed arrows, Cupid's quiver with arrows. In carpets these designs could be found in central round or oval motifs or at the corners. At one time Madame de Pompadour invested in an import firm, Compagnie des Indes, and to make the venture profitable she insisted that everyone espouse all things Oriental. The result was a profusion of Chinoiserie—oriental ladies with parasols, gazebos, singerie, and misty mountains appeared painted on boiserie and furniture, or were woven into textiles (to a lesser extent into carpet designs).

Each succeeding king was in moderate revolt against the established fashion of his predecessor. As Louis XIV espoused classicism in the grand Baroque manner, and Louis XV the romanticism of the Rococo, so Louis XVI (1774–1793), a man of sensitive taste, created a restrained, balanced architectural form on an intimate scale, indicating that refinement and delicacy were more important than strength. Straight lines replaced the Rococo curve. Unfortunately, Louis XVI inherited with his crown a somewhat depleted treasury, a high rate of unemployment, and a population rapidly growing disenchanted with absolute monarchy.

Louis XVI was immature and of weak character for all of his great taste. He had the dubious fortune of having been married to an equally child-like bride, the pretty and charming Marie Antoinette of Austria. Together they played through life unaware of the storm brewing outside the palace walls. Marie Antoinette chose to play the role of a fresh young milkmaid and had built near the Petit Trianon (a gift from her husband) an enchanting miniature Swiss village. Here she and her ladies-in-waiting pretended the innocent pleasures of the peasant country life, picnicking amid laces, silks, ribbons, large straw bonnets, and a profusion of flowers. Three court painters, Boucher, Greuze, and Fragonard have amply documented these picturesque games of nobles and courtiers.

Textile patterns, and in particular the patterns of Aubusson and Savon-nerie carpets, echoed the pale delicacy of these paintings. Woven among the flower patterns were forms of garden tools, sunbonnets, bouquets of flowers tied with long floating ribbons, cartouches in pale delicate colors. Coquilles, classic scrolls, the Greek key and acanthus leaves appeared in corners and border patterns. The classic egg and dart or dentil moldings outlined the border patterns. The neoclassic style was a strong fashion force despite the crumbling of the social order which created it. While Marie Antoinette was bemusing herself and friends, Voltaire and Rousseau were enflaming the French population to revolt, and the self-indulgent reign of Marie Antoinette and Louis XVI came to a violent end while he was still in his mid-thirties.

France then suffered her worst revolution—a period of great strife and destruction. Industry, and in particular that of the building and decorative crafts, abruptly came to a halt. It was not until 1804, when Napoleon I became emperor (after a series of successful campaigns against Austria and Holland) that the country began to rebuild and decorate with its former gusto. Napoleon created a new aristocracy and a new distribution of wealth. These *nouveaux riches* unfortunately had neither the wit nor sophistication of the earlier elite but they did surround themselves with a certain luxury. This new period was called Empire.

During the interim years of the revolution and the First Empire, the country witnessed several transitional governments—the First Republic (1792–1795), the Directory (1795–1799), and the Consulate (1799–1804). These were all short term governments—periods of reorganization which had only a fleeting effect on the decorative crafts.

Directoire and Consulate styles were manifested by symbols of war—spears, banners, the twelve sticks of Rome tied with ribbons, and cartouches. Architecture and furniture became simplified, symbolizing the new spirit of nationalism. Motifs were taken from Pompeiian and classic Greek forms. But it was the age of Napoleon, the Empire, in which classicism revisited frankly became identified. Like Louis XIV, Napoleon set up a system of state supervision unifying the arts. Percier and Fontaine became the architects of a style calculated to recreate the grandeur of Rome, somewhat less of Greece. The ancient themes of modified warlike symbols took precedence. Woven into silks and magnificent carpets were the forms of swords, shields, helmets, and flaming torches, (*flambeaux*). The style invaded England to become Regency and America as American Empire.

Pale, delicate colors gave way to masculine browns, violets, olive greens, emerald greens, royal blues, and deep wine reds highlighted with gold. Gold threads were woven into fabrics. Furniture had applied mounts of heavy gold ormulu and bronze. In a later campaign in Italy, Napoleon discovered the partially restored city of Pompeii. He developed a passion for its classic forms found in the furniture and architecture and later, when home in Paris, he commanded his ebonists and weavers to incorporate many of the decorative forms and motifs of Pompeii into his household furnishings. The letter N became entwined with laurel leaf wreaths (the Roman symbol of the athlete) or sometimes alternated with the bumblebee (an early symbol of industry and also incorporated in the Bonaparte crest). Narrow classical architectural borders appeared, edging or framing other leafy borders, urns, sphinx heads, lions, and the Italian cornucopia (symbol of plenty), garlands, and the fleur-de-lys. To these multitudes of designs, Josephine, the first wife of Napoleon, added her particular favorite, the swan. Marie Louise, his second wife, had a peculiar veneration for the poor little Marie Antoinette, her tragic aunt, and she revived the floral carpets of the eighteenth century. Under the patronage of Napoleon the tapestry and rug industries of Aubusson and Savonnerie were revived. Early cartoons and looms had been destroyed during the Revolution and in the years which followed, the centers virtually went out of business.

It was a short term reprieve, however, for soon after the craftsmen's mentor was banished to Elba in disgrace, the workshops at Aubusson and Beauvais began to diversify. The power loom, already used successfully in England, was invading France, and those traditional handweaving centers capitulated to the easier and surely swifter method of weaving. The Wilton

Loom by that time had been perfected to produce asymmetrical patterns of flowers and rosettes.

By the middle of the nineteenth century a new society was growing up in France, the bourgeois, a wealthy middle class. They were practical people. They had not been spoiled by the refinements of the handwoven tapestry and carpet; for them a copy would do just as well. Needlework was becoming a popular pastime for the ladies and some of the best rugs of the period were executed by those ladies who found it amusing to express themselves in this kind of handiwork.

For the first time style was lacking in invention; there was a general lack of direction and self confidence. This was not due so much to a lack of ability on the part of the craftsman but to a reluctance to attempt to create anything of quality. The material wants of a vast majority of people having been attended to, it was now comfort and convenience they craved.

Change and variety rather than performance became virtues. The machine reproduced adequate and attractive merchandise, however hybrid, with enough acceptable styles for all tastes. The decorator and his client merely needed to exercise choice in the matter. No one was confined to a single style; individuality and the restless search for novelty seemed to give much satisfaction to both the decorator and his client in the search for a new personal status. The result was a mild state of design chaos.

It may be that machine-made rugs and carpets, resulting in endless inferior copies, played the largest part in the general demise of the hand weaving and knotting industry, but by the first decade of the twentieth century, weaving in the traditional centers virtually came to a halt.

During the 1890's a style called Art Nouveau swept the continent. The name was taken from a small shop by the same name which opened in Paris on the Rue de Provence by a M. S. Bing in 1895. This style was in reaction to the machine. The movement closely followed the Arts and Crafts movement of the British artist-craftsman, William Morris. It was illustrated by growing plant forms with exuberant curling and twisting tendrils and attenuated lilies, tulips and other flowers. The effect, however, was one of fused balance and coherent form. The rather voluptuous and highly complex patterns printed on fabrics were recreated in a few carpets and rugs. Some still exist.

Following closely on the heels of this Art Nouveau philosophy which negated the machine, was Art Moderne (1919), or more specifically the French interpretation of the international Bauhaus philosophy of Gropius, which dictated that design could be made compatible for machine manufacture. In woven textiles and carpets this manifested itself in a severity of line—a careful balance of solid colors and lines. Patterns assumed a defined, almost non-representational, geometric appearance.

During the twenties, there was an effort to revive the hand weaving crafts and to re-establish the Aubusson and Gobelin (formerly Savonnerie) centers. The object was to create modern designs for an ancient craft. The group of artists involved was headed by artist Jean Lurçat, an enthusiastic embroiderer, and included Gromaire, Dufy, and Matisse. They hoped to recreate a sense of fantasy, which the Gothic tapestries possessed, within modern terms. This was to give man a sense of relief from the regulated business world. A few tapestry weavers were assembled and wove tapestries and a limited number of carpets with great delicacy and refinement. Later other artists, including several Americans, designed cartoons to be translated into tapestries. A few small rugs have emerged from this effort—all originals and all "signed" by the artist in limited editions. They, too, represent the craft at its best. Activity in these centers continues today.

Savonnerie

The Savonnerie carpet, aristocrat of carpets of the Western world, was first produced in 1628. This type of carpet has a textured pile, knotted by hand in much the same manner as an Oriental carpet, with a Turkish knot. Savonnerie carpets are usually baronial in size and are better suited to elaborate and formal rooms. The scale of the pattern is always in keeping with the size of the carpet. In many cases patterns in rich and strong colors are so naturalistic one almost hesitates to step on them. The warp of flax (linen) is strung on a vertical loom and the pile has raised loops of thick wool yarns. To accelerate the knotting, the pattern-forming pile yarns (or weft) are wound around a thin iron rod that terminates in a sharp blade. As the rod is pulled out, the pile loops are cut apart. Rows of these cut pile yarns are alternated with several rows of plain weft tightly pressed into pile (or weft) to hold them together. Later, to accentuate the central and border patterns, a little of the edge of the main field is hand cut or beveled, leaving a slightly carved appearance.

Documents date the opening of the Savonnerie factory in 1628. There is slight discrepancy or confusion, however, about the inventor of the French

Savonnerie type weave. Pierre DuPont, who was established at the Louvre, claims to have created the process in 1604. Jean Poitier made a similar claim at approximately the same time. It has been generally conceded that DuPont was the father of the Savonnerie weave, which takes its name from the second home of the factory, a defunct soap factory. This was located in Chaillot, at the time a fashionable suburb, now a part of Paris. The move was taken not long after the original looms had been set up within the huge complex of the Louvre, a space they quickly outgrew.

Prior to the move, the soap factory had become a hospice and children's home and one of the basic reasons for establishing a factory there, in fact, was to give financial aid, through rents, to the struggling hospice. An apprentice system for the children would, on the other hand, supply an unlimited source of trained weavers. Each young boy living at the hospice worked as an apprentice for eight years. At the end of twelve years, if he continued to pursue the trade, he received a lump sum of money in payment for his activities. The training must have been rigid and the children talented, for after some years the Savonnerie factory turned out the most beautiful carpets of the finest quality found anywhere.

Pierre DuPont was undoubtedly exposed as a boy to the Saracenic weavers at the court of Charles IX, for he had a rare and mature understanding of the art of weaving. In 1604 he wrote an essay on the subject "La Stromatourgie," which he presented to the reigning Henry IV. The original of this essay is still preserved at the Bibliothèque Nationale in Paris.

Henry IV was enough impressed with the treatise to create the title of Court Weaver for DuPont. He set up looms for him in a corner of the Louvre. By 1624, these quarters became crowded and DuPont made an agreement with one of his associates, Simon Lourdet, to divide the looms. Lourdet established his share at the small but functioning center at the Savonnerie. To protect their art and in particular their own two factories—the one at the Louvre and the one at the Savonnerie—they asked for, and received, protection from the crown. This was in the form of a guarantee that no carpets, Oriental or other type of foreign make, would be imported into the city of Paris. As an extra proviso, the French weavers would be allowed to travel to foreign lands in search of wool and dyes. This protection was granted by Henry IV and lasted eighteen years.

DuPont died in 1650 and his son Philippe (who died shortly after) inherited the looms located in the Louvre. After the death of Simon Lourdet, the young DuPont moved his looms to the hospice, where he and Madame

Lourdet established a partnership. In 1661 Madame Lourdet made a large carpet for the young King Louis XIV, who had not as yet reached his majority but was reigning under the regency of his mother, Anne of Austria. Later, when Louis XIV came of age, he ordered ninety important carpets for the Grand Gallery of the Louvre. These were completed in 1684 and Madame Lourdet realized more than one half-million dollars from this commission. The carpets were large, measuring approximately 16' 10" by 30' long. In 1688, the King of Siam placed a ninety thousand dollar order for two large and sumptuous carpets. In the same year the Pope commissioned several carpets for his suite at Fontainebleau. It was, in fact, a period of economic stability within the country, which lasted until the middle of the reign of Louis XV. It was also a period of great nationalism and all styles were uniquely French, devoid of outside design influences.

When Louis XV inherited the crown, he changed the existing large rooms at both the Louvre and Versailles, breaking them up into smaller, more intimate spaces. During this change, the looms at the Savonnerie were kept busy to such an extent that no commissions outside of those specifically marked for the crown could be honored. This state of affairs continued through the reign of Louis XVI and into the trying period of Revolution in 1789, at which time all work ceased. It was not until the First Empire, when Napoleon was crowned emperor, that work resumed with any kind of regularity. Then a number of carpets for the Tuileries, including the throne room, were commissioned. Many of the classic styles of ancient Rome and Pompeii were adapted to carpets.

In 1825, the Savonnerie factory formally moved its looms to the Manufacture Nationale des Gobelins, a tapestry weaving and wool dyeing center in Paris. This was the official state factory first established under the direction of Henry IV, later purchased by Colbert for Louis XIV. The weaving of Savonnerie carpets has intermittently continued there ever since.

Today the word Savonnerie means a type or style of weave, and carpets woven in this manner can be found to emanate from many other parts of the world.

Aubusson

The name Aubusson comes from a small town in the Creuse Valley near Limoges, France. There was, and still is, an organized industry but no factory;

for Aubusson is a center of individual weavers all adhering to a strict form or style of weaving construction. Carpets made in this manner have no pile and are woven with a traditional thick-thread tapestry weave on looms. Until the nineteenth century the warp was a combination of flax (linen) and wool. After the nineteenth century, it became cotton. The weft, or fill, threads have always been of wool in various colors.

No one knows when weaving started in this area, but it is certain that tapestries were woven there long before the Gothic era. Early documented carpet designs were, like the Spanish, influenced by the Oriental carpet— mainly those of Saracenic origin. Later, during Gothic times, carpets were patterned with *mille fleurs* as were the background designs of many tapestries. Many of the weavers who settled in France were Huguenots who had fled Spain during the Inquisition of the early sixteenth century. Later in the same century Henry IV, himself a Huguenot, established paternal protection over these weavers by issuing the Edict of Nantes, granting all non-Catholics freedom of worship. The decrees against foreign imports, also established by Henry IV, protecting those weavers at the Louvre and the Savonnerie, applied also to the weavers in Aubusson.

The Aubusson weavers were great craftsmen but they were not fine artists. Designs were stimulated by outside sources; cartoons were drawn or painted which the craftsmen copied with the most incredible finesse. There were no finer craftsmen in the world. Because of the quality, royalty chose to commission designs to be woven by them rather than at such outside sources as Brussels and Flanders. During the reign of Louis XIV both Aubusson and Gobelin (tapestry) weaving centers claimed the title of Royal Manufactory, but at Aubusson the quality of dyeing and weaving had not quite attained the fine performance it later developed. It was Louis XIV who sent his Prime Minister, Colbert, to Flanders to find artists to create designs specially suited for carpets and to instruct the young aspiring weavers to refine their standard of performance. Specially trained dyers were also brought to Aubusson. A long and hard apprenticeship was established to obtain the title, Master of Tapestry.

Like the Savonnerie, all activity at Aubusson virtually halted during the Revolution in 1789. For a short period during the First Empire (the decorative period is placed 1804–1820) some activity was evident, but in France the taste for quality in all household furnishings was diminishing and the need for hand woven tapestries and carpets was extremely limited.

It was not until well into the 1920's that an artist and embroiderer, Jean Lurçat, and a group of prominent artists revived the art of the tapestry weave at Aubusson. Prior to that a few craftsmen had trained sporadically in the center but original works of art were not forthcoming. Instead they recreated a number of old, and often times partially destroyed, cartoons of an earlier period. Where the pattern was missing some attempt was made to patch new drawings or bits of other drawings together, which led to a decidedly inferior product. Under the tutelage of Lurçat, new designs created by himself and his group—Miro, Dufy, Matisse, Gromaire, and still later, Picard le Douce and Mategot—were woven. The quality once again resembled that of the old days.

Today the center at Aubusson, now under the control of the French Ministry of Arts, is a busy village turning out tapestries and an occasional carpet of the finest quality. Designs come from painters in all parts of the world, including the United States.

Gobelins

The original Manufacture Nationale des Gobelins in the weaving center of Beauvais was established by the Gobelin dyers of Rheims. Under Henry IV, a group of the Gobelin dyers and Beauvais weavers set up a center in Paris to create, for the numerous châteaux built by the king, a large number of tapestries. But the fame of the center was developed during the reign of Louis XIV, when Colbert, under the king's direction, bought the center for royal use. Artist-decorator LeBrun personally guided the creations of the center. The weaving capacity was greatly increased. Unfortunately the history of this illustrious tapestry center suffers from the same political crises as its companion centers at Aubusson and Savonnerie. Carpets were not woven here until 1825, when the Savonnerie factory closed its doors to join this group.

Today the Gobelin manufactory boasts not only its fine weaving factory, but a dye shop, a laboratory for developing new dyes, a museum, a school, and a laboratory for the restoration of old tapestries.

French, Louis XIII. Savonnerie. *Courtesy of Hamot, Paris.*

France, Louis XIV. Savonnerie, second half XVII century. Coat of arms of Colbert. Above is the decoration of Saint Esprit. *Courtesy Musée des Arts Decoratil.*

France, Louis XIV. Savonnerie circa 1660. *Courtesy Musée des Arts Décoratifs.*

French. Savonnerie, 1660–1680. *Musée Nissim de Camondo, Paris.*

Opposite page:

Top, left: French, Louis XIV. Savonnerie, 1673–1681, wool. *The Metropolitan Museum of Art, Gift of the Samuel H. Kress Foundation, 1958.*

Top, right: French, Louis XIV. Center medallion. *The Metropolitan Museum of Art.*

French, Louis XIV. Detail of above right. Figure of woman with lion. *The Metropolitan Museum of Art.*

French. Savonnerie, 1680–1690. *Musée Nissim de Camondo, Paris.*

Top: French, Louis XIV, probably 1685–1697. Savonnerie, wool. *The Metropolitan Museum of Art, Rogers Fund, 1952.*

Above: Detail of top picture.

Left: Detail of top picture.

French, Louis XIV, late 17th century style. Aubusson (detail). *Courtesy of Parke-Bernet Galleries.*

French, Louis XIV. Savonnerie, late 17th century. *Courtesy of Hamot, Paris.*

French, needlepoint, late 17th century style. *Courtesy of Parke-Bernet Galleries.*

French, probably Regence, early 18th century. Savonnerie. *Courtesy of Hamot, Paris.*

French, Louis XV, Savonnerie. Cartoon. *Courtesy of Hamot, Paris.*

Above: French, Louis XV. Sa-
vonnerie, mid-18th century.
Cartoon. *Courtesy of Hamot,
Paris.*

Right: French, rare Louis XV.
Aubusson, mid-18th century.
Courtesy of Hamot, Paris.

Opposite page:

Top: French, circa 1740. Savonnerie. *Musée Nissim de
Camondo, Paris.*

French, circa 1745. Savonnerie.
*Musée Nissim de Camondo,
Paris.*

French, Louis XVI style. *Courtesy of Parke-Bernet Galleries.*

French. Aubusson, 1760–1770. Au point de Savonnerie. *Musée Nissim de Camondo, Paris.*

French, 1760. Savonnerie. Pour Mesdames de France, pour la Chapelle de Versailles. *Musée Nissim de Camondo, Paris.*

Left: French, Louis XVI. Savonnerie. Palace carpet, showing corner detail. *Courtesy of Parke-Bernet Galleries.*

French, circa 1770. Savonnerie. *Musée Nissim de Camondo, Paris.*

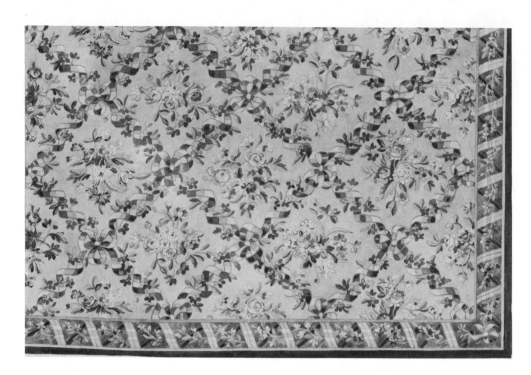

French, rare Louis XVI. Aubusson, late 18th century. Partial carpet. *Courtesy of Hamot, Paris.*

French, Louis XVI. Savonnerie, late 18th century. Cartoon detail. *Courtesy of Hamot, Paris.*

French, Louis XVI. Savonnerie, late 18th century. *Courtesy of Hamot, Paris.*

French, Louis XVI style. Savonnerie, late 18th century. *Courtesy of Parke-Bernet Galleries.*

Left: French, Louis XVI. Savonnerie, late 18th century. *Courtesy of Hamot, Paris.*

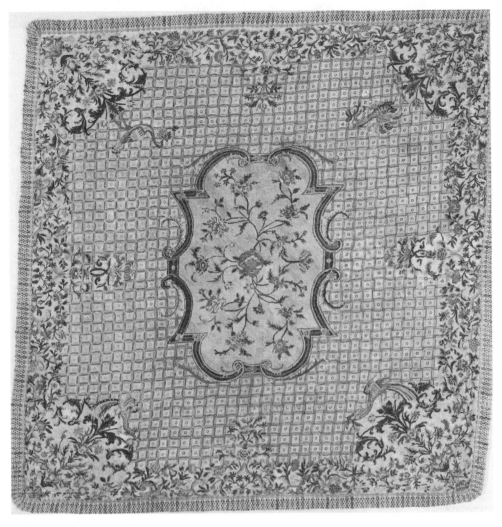

French, 18th century. Silk embroidered on canvas. *The Metropolitan Museum of Art, Gift of Mary Hayward Wier, 1965.*

French, Louis XVI. Savonnerie, circa 1790. *Courtesy of Parke-Bernet Galleries.*

French. Aubusson, circa 1790. Au point de Savonnerie. *Musée Nissim de Camondo, Paris.*

French, Directoire: 1795–1799. Savonnerie. *Courtesy of Hamot, Paris.*

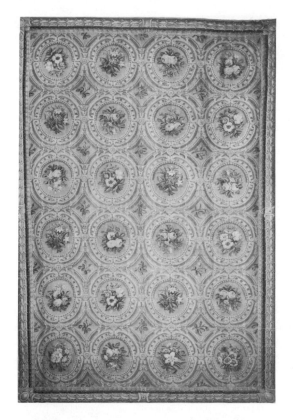

French, Directoire: 1799. Aubusson. *Courtesy of Parke-Bernet Galleries.*

French, Restoration. Savonnerie. *Courtesy of Hamot, Paris.*

French, rare Restoration. Aubusson. *Courtesy of Hamot, Paris.*

French Empire. Savonnerie. *Courtesy of Hamot, Paris.*

French, Restoration. *The Metropolitan Museum of Art, Gift of Captain and Mrs. W. C. Fitch, 1910, in memory of Clyde Fitch.*

French Empire. Aubusson (detail). *Courtesy of Parke-Bernet Galleries, Berberyan Collection.*

French Empire. Savonnerie (detail). *Courtesy of Hamot, Paris.*

Left: French, Charles X, circa 1825. Aubusson (detail). *Courtesy of Parke-Bernet Galleries, Private Collection.*

Opposite page: French, Charles X, circa 1825. *Courtesy of Parke-Bernet Galleries, Berberyan Collection.*

French, reproduction of an original Charles X carpet. Aubusson. *Courtesy of Parke-Bernet Galleries, Berberyan Collection.*

French, reproduction of a Charles X carpet circa 1825. *Courtesy of Parke-Bernet Galleries, Berberyan Collection.*

French, Louis Philippe, circa 1830. *Courtesy of Parke-Bernet Galleries, Private Collection.*

French, Louis Philippe, circa 1845. *Courtesy of Parke-Bernet Galleries, Private Collection.*

French, Louis Philippe, circa 1835. Aubusson. *Courtesy of Parke-Bernet Galleries, Private Collection.*

Opposite page: French, Louis Philippe, circa 1830. Aubusson. *Courtesy of Parke-Bernet Galleries, Private Collection.*

French, circa 1900, wool carpet. *The Metropolitan Museum of Art, Gift of Mr. Robert Armstrong, 1958.*

Left: French, Louis Philippe, circa 1840. Aubusson.

French, 20th century (first quarter). *The Metropolitan Museum of Art, Purchase 1925, Edward C. Moore, Jr.*

French, 20th century (?). French needlepoint medallion carpet. *Courtesy of Parke-Bernet Galleries, Berberyan Collection.*

Opposite page: French, 20th century. Aubusson. Reproduction of an original in Lady Mendl's Trianon Cottage at Versailles. *Courtesy of Parke-Bernet Galleries, Berberyan Collection.*

French, 20th century (?). Point d'Hongrie embroidered rug. *Courtesy of Parke-Bernet Galleries, Berberyan Collection.*

French. Aubusson. *Courtesy of French Government Tourist Office.*

French, Victorian, 20th century. Needlepoint carpet. *Courtesy of Parke-Bernet Galleries, Berberyan Collection.*

French Empire. Library of Malmaison. *Courtesy of French Government Tourist Office.*

French Empire. Chambre de L' Emperatrice, Palais de Fontainebleau. *Courtesy of French Government Tourist Office.*

French. Palais de Fontainebleau. Salon François I. *Courtesy of French Government Tourist Office.*

Opposite page:

Top: French Empire. Palais de Fontainebleau. Chambre de Napoléon. *Courtesy of French Government Tourist Office.*

French. Palais de Fontainebleau. *Courtesy of French Government Tourist Office.*

3 GREAT BRITAIN

English, Elizabethan. "Lucretia's Banquet," wool and silk on canvas in tent stitch. *Victoria and Albert Museum. Lord Willoughby de Broke Collection.*

COUNTRY HOUSES and the good country life were a unique expression of the English nobility and rich bourgeois. The arts and crafts of the country were developed mainly not for royalty, but for a small group, these country elite and a handful of Londoners who demanded something a little different with each successive era. They were adventurous, not in the least shy in experimenting with new styles of architecture and accepting inventive expressions of foreign artists and craftsmen.

Although architecture was advanced, for centuries little consideration was given to interior furnishings, until the Late Georgian Period when the Adam brothers, in particular Robert, introduced the pleasures of the "compleat" room—a room where interior decorations were a discreet extension and fulfillment of the architectural surroundings. In the case of the Adams, the style was severely classical.

Early in the Tudor Period (1500–1603) the country was small, barely exceeding three million people. The majority lived in the country, many in villages clustered around manor houses, on prosperous farms, or near markets centers. Where corn, the prevailing crop, would not grow, flocks of sheep were raised. In towns and country alike a rising wool-textile industry was developing, and for generations raw or carded wool was England's major export. But it was not until the end of the fifteenth century that finished cloth was woven for export. Until then, weaving had been considered a menial task, the work of farmers' wives who wove the cloth, cut, and sewed it for clothing.

England's contribution was not its exports but was directed toward its great expansion through colonization, and its judicial system based on democratic thinking, with an ensuing justice of order, industry, and progress, much admired and copied by a number of nations.

The English nature, a result of its Nordic ancestry (Celts, Saxons, Danes, and Normans), was austere, and among average men there was an instinctive abhorrence of a sybaritic display of worldly goods. This was clearly demonstrated in 1252 in London, when the population of the city turned out to greet the young Spanish princess, bride of the Prince of Wales, later Edward I. The young lady, Eleanor of Castile, sister of Alphonse X, had brought with her a dowry which included many regal Oriental carpets, and in the Spanish manner had lined her private rooms in Westminster with these richly decorated carpets, not only to display their beauty but to keep out the cold. Londoners were not impressed. To the contrary, it seems they were acutely embarrassed for the young wife who required such comfort. (In later years it is quite possible that Eleanor gave several of her carpets to Westminster Abbey, for listed in the Abbey records dated 1388 there appears, among a number of entries, one grass-green cloth with the arms of England, Spain, and of Queen Eleanor.)

These carpets were not the first to appear in England, however, for history tells us that prior to the year 992, Egebric, Abbott of Croyden, commissioned two large "fote cloths," handwoven with lions, to be used before the altar on festive days. But in general, carpets and rugs were unknown five hundred years ago. In France and Spain, their adoption kept pace with a progressive idea of comfort and luxury, but in England practically nothing was known of the pile carpet until the reign of Edward I, husband of the unpopular Spanish bride, nor were they generally accepted as part of the interior design scheme until late in the reign of Elizabeth I in the sixteenth century.

The earliest floor coverings were rushes spread over earthen or tiled floors. The practice was to scatter them over the floor renewing them from time to time. In some sections of the country rushes were alternated with straw, hay, foliage, fragrant herbs, or flowers, and were renewed daily. The reasons were hygienic, however, rather than esthetic. The practice continued sometime after the reign of Elizabeth I (1558–1603). As late as 1598 a German traveler noted in a letter to a friend that the Queen had received her visitors (in Greenwich) "in a chamber strewn with hay."

With few exceptions, carpets were not mentioned or documented again until the sixteenth century when Cardinal Wolsey, as Chancellor and close confidant of Henry VIII, undoubtedly the first Englishman to consider them an important part of the interior scene, obtained a few for his personal use. Rumor had it that Wolsey had aspirations to the papal crown, and fed by dreams of grandeur, he felt it necessary to establish himself arbiter of continental fashion as well as diplomacy. As his tastes were advanced beyond those of his neighbors and beyond the creative capacities of craftsmen in his own country, he was forced to turn to other countries for many household luxuries.

The hub of the Eastern trade at the time was through a group of Venetian factors in London with whom Wolsey was angry, and upon whom he had imposed a stiff tariff on wines and spices, a Venetian monopoly. To placate him, Sabastian Giustinian, the Venetian Ambassador, attempted to bribe Wolsey with the promise of a gift of seven fine Damascene carpets. In June of 1518 Giustinian wrote from Lambeth to his Signory in Venice that the Cardinal had promised to obtain for him (Giustinian) an audience with the British Council to enable the Venetians to present arguments for the repeal of the tax. Giustinian added in his letter

. . . I did not know whether there were any (carpets) but that if there were, his Lordship would have them. I suspect he will not be accommodated which will prove a serious detriment to us, whereas had he received 12 or 15 small handsome carpets, he would have been extremely satisfied.

In November of the same year Giustinian again wrote to Venice that ". . . the Cardinal was extremely angry with the Venetian merchants in London who, he felt, did not seriously consider his request for carpets and who took his political influence in Parliament too lightly."

In the end, it seems, the Venetian government, being unable or unwilling to produce the carpets, forced the Venetians in London into purchasing the carpets themselves. Giustinian sold a gold chain given him by Henry VIII and some gold cups, a gift from the King of Hungary. Others did the same, and by October 1520, Wolsey finally received some sixty carpets of Oriental make from Venice.

Hampton Court, the Cardinal's home, was typical of early Tudor architecture—essentially Gothic with applied decoration—in this case Italianate ornament, the work of immigrant architect Giovanni de Maiano, who was employed by Wolsey. The house was of lavish proportions, with ample room in which to receive such a staggering number of carpets in the vivid and ornate Oriental style. Indeed Hampton Court far outdistanced Westminster, the home of Henry VIII, who in a fit of jealousy deposed his high and mighty Cardinal. Nonetheless, Wolsey carpets did start a new fashion among the nobility.

Prior to the Venetian incident, some attempt had been made under Wolsey's direction to establish an industry for the hand knotting (in Oriental manner) of small pile rugs. In 1509 William Sheldon established a tapestry works at Barchester, Warwickshire, and it was believed a few rugs were woven there as well as at a similar establishment at Ramsey. In Ramsey a kind of imitation French "Arras" (French tapestry woven in Flemish manner) was being woven on horizontal looms, which somewhat resembled hand-knotted originals but which were, in fact, a good deal cheaper because of the inferior weave. But in general hand knotting, a tedious job, met with little success among English craftsmen. The production of a true Oriental or "Turkey" carpet meant building or importing upright looms instead of trying to adapt horizontal looms built for weaving heavy cloth. Only a few of these newer-type hand looms appeared in areas where wool was produced. Robert Rothe, Earl of Ormond, imported both looms and weavers from the East in order to make a large Turkey carpet on his estate at Kilkenny in 1539.

The word "Turkey" was loosely used by the English to denote any imported type of colorful Oriental carpet hand-knotted in the Turkish manner with the Ghiordes knot. Later, the word "Turkey" also encompassed the many domestically hand-knotted or woven reproductions. "Turkey" and an equally ubiquitous word, "Holbein," became synonymous when speaking of Orientals—they became generic terms. Originally "Holbein" carpet described a type which appeared in many of the portraits painted by Hans Holbein.

Henry VIII, the least insular of early English monarchs, invited a number of European artists—painters and architects—to work in England. Among them was the Flemish painter, Hans Holbein, who subsequently became court painter. The many portraits of the royal family and of nobles remain the best reference for interior furnishings of important homes of the day. In the background of a number of these Holbein paintings are small rugs used to decorate tables, a popular use for luxurious and beautiful Orientals of the time. It is most possible that these rugs were imports, but it could be true that certain carpets were reproductions, made to order at various small or private weaving establishments somewhere in England.

Many of these so-called Holbein carpets had patterns of angular arabesques designed in rows of strap-work alternating with octagonals or diamond shapes, rather like patterns of the modern Bokhara carpet. Some appeared with borders of Kufic lettering. It would seem that the Oriental or the domestic reproduction of the Oriental was so popular that no attempt was made by English weavers to develop any other style more identifiable with the English nature.

During the early Tudor Period, carpet imports were on the increase, due mainly to England's ever-broadening merchant shipping fleets and an easing of the accesses to Middle Eastern ports via the Mediterranean. It was only after the imprudent divorce of Henry VIII and his Spanish wife, Catherine of Aragon, followed by Henry's establishment of a lenient Church of England that Catholic countries, in particular Spain, blocked passage to English fleets attempting to enter those ports. This state of affairs lasted until 1588 when Sir Francis Drake, in the name of "good" Queen Elizabeth liberated the sea routes into the Mediterranean by defeating the Spanish Armada.

During that interim, a serious attempt was made to expand a domestic carpet weaving industry to satisfy a growing demand for handsome, warm carpets for wealthy households. Wool was plentiful and labor inexpensive. Products made in England became cheaper than early Asian imports. And as the craft spread, a domestic style began to become noticeable. It manifested itself with brightly colored floral patterns reminiscent of that exuberant flora of the English country garden. Nobility commissioned weavers to weave carpets with heraldic designs set among Oriental or floral motifs. One such knotted carpet, bearing three coats of arms dated 1570, appeared in the collection of the Earl of Verulam at Gorhambury, while others appeared in inventories of Queen Elizabeth I in the Borough of Ipswich, and again in the Harbottle family. The designs of these carpets were surrounded by a sort of diaper pattern. The border had a typically English naturalistic honeysuckle trail. Several domestic Holbein or Turkey rugs were also inventoried at about the same time including one with a typically Turkish coloration, but woven into it were the arms of Sir Edward Apsley (knighted in 1603) with an inscription which reads . . . "FEARE GOD, AND KEEPE HIS COM-MANDMENTS/MADE IN THE YEAR 1603."

Many of these fresh patterns looked like early hand embroideries. For centuries needlework had been one of the favorite occupations of wives and daughters of families living isolated in the countryside. Even Mathilde, wife of William the Conqueror, was said to have created the famous Bayeux tapestry while waiting for her husband to return from the battlefield. But it was the delightful light and brightly colored threads these women used for their handiwork which finally influenced the colorations and patterns peculiar to the English hand-knotted and woven rugs and carpets. The ladies' "Turkie" work rugs, as this type of needlework was sometimes called, involved an enormous amount of work and time. Many had thick piles (mainly reds, green, or blue). But the rugs were barely able to stand hard wear; they were more like embroideries used to decorate a floor on festive occasions. Some made during the sixteenth century still exist in private collections today.

Naturalistic flowers abounded over the face of many of these collectors' rugs or embroideries in such profusion that connecting scrolls, stems, or tendrils completely disappeared. Pansies, the favorite of Queen Elizabeth I, were particularly popular. Worms and winged insects (probably inspired by the Gothic *mille fleurs* tapestries) appeared. Borders repeated with Oriental-like patterns had cartouches in corners, and on occasion, the initials ER (Elizabeth Regina) or a date.

The designs and color remained quite individual, but the simplicity of the floral style was considered primitive in comparison with the elaborate and florid patterns found in France and Spain. Those patterns tended to bewilder the more austere English, who simply could not assimilate them. It was not until the seventeenth century that the more sophisticated English could enjoy the Baroque style—by that time *passé* on the continent. But simple and refreshing as these English hand-woven or embroidered rug styles were, they were the forerunners of the more elaborate factory hand-knotted or woven carpets which today we recognize as the English style.

Toward the end of the reign of Elizabeth I, the English-Turkey (or Levant) Company had begun direct trading with the Middle Eastern shores of the Mediterranean, and once again carpets from those Asian ports became easier to obtain. Of those, many were more or less faithfully copied by the growing number of small factories springing up around the English country-side.

According to a sixteenth-century guide, Hakluyt's *Voyages*,

. . . certain directions were given to (a) Mr. M. Hubblethorne, D'ier, sent to Persia 1579 . . . you shall finde carpets of coarse thrummed wool, the best in the world, and excellently coloured; those cities and towns you must repair to and you must use all means to learn all the order of the dying of those thrums, which so dyed as neither rain, wine, nor yet vinegar can stain . . . If before you return you could procure a singular good worker in the arts of Turkish carpet making, you should bring the man to the realm, and also thereby increase work to your own company.

A few years later carpets were, it seems, hand-woven or knotted by Persians under the direction of Mr. Hubblethorne at Norwich. These had cotton or flax (linen) warps with wefts (or fill) of wool.

The Stuart or Jacobean Age (1603–1714) was an era of national expansion. No longer could Britain call itself a "tight little island." By now it encompassed England, Scotland, Wales, and Ireland. By the time of the death of Queen Anne (1714), England was a powerful Western European nation, joined to France not only by political ties but through marriage. (The tragic Scot, Charles I, married Henrietta Marie of France.) The English took to emulating French manners, decoration, fashion, and the literary arts. The English were also discovering the classic worlds of Greece and Rome. Added to this newborn interest in the beauties of architecture and the decorative arts, importers were tantalizing the public with Florentine silks, and Indian chintzes. As the awareness for decorative living grew, it became natural, if not necessary, that some less expensive floor covering, priced for the moderate pocketbook, be developed on existing looms—the treadle-operated horizontal looms traditionally used to weave heavy cloths. Looms offered a faster process than the painstaking hand-knotting process.

The center of the broadcloth industry was in Kidderminster and there an attempt was made to weave coarser wool, unsuitable for clothing, into a type of floor covering. The result was a dullish flat-woven goods called "fote cloths." Although the result was undistinguished, the process by which this material was woven was the first attempt to develop a carpet weaving machine which could help to broaden the industry, capable of weaving quantities of carpeting for the majority of people. The process spread to Wilton (1655), and to Mortlake (now a section of London).

Following the revocation of the Edict of Nantes in 1685, many of the sixty thousand French Huguenots who fled to England seeking religious freedom were weavers, and quite naturally they gravitated to those established weaving centers. Their fresh ideas became a catalyst for newer weaving techniques. In one case the addition of extra heddles and a weft box for the horizontal loom enabled the weaver to create a patterned flat-weave carpet. In another, at Kidderminster, the loom was adjusted in such a manner as to weave a reversible or double-cloth carpet.

Weaving centers at Kidderminster, Mortlake, Wilton, and Norwich soon became so successful that rival factories with less skilled weavers sprang up around the countryside. The total lack of supervision or performance standard became so acute, and the need to protect the legitimate factory became so great, that William III (1694–1702) was forced to draw up a charter in 1701 to protect the skilled weaver. (The charter was renewed in 1706 and again in 1725.) An association of weavers was formed and certificates were issued to all who had served a seven-year apprenticeship. This quickly put an end to the fly-by-night factories. And by the end of the eighteenth century, carpet weaving in England had become a recognized industry.

In 1730, Lord Pembroke visited the Savonnerie factories in France, where he found not only the great royal carpets being hand-knotted on upright looms in the traditional manner, but he found Tournai or Brussels loop-pile carpets of a superior quality being woven on treadle-operated horizontal looms. The work was so impressive he was determined to import several workers to his family seat, Wilton. Unfortunately, French law prohibited the export of skilled craftsmen and, according to Bertram Jacobs in his handbook, *The Story of British Carpets*, a legend (which Jacobs finds hard to believe) exists today at Wilton that Pembroke smuggled two men out of France in two empty wine barrels among a cargo of Burgundy wine. The truth is, however, that an Anthony Dufossy and a Peter Jemaule (whose names might very well have been Antoine and Pierre) arrived at Wilton in 1720 and set up the first Brussels looms there. Their descendants still live in the area.

Although much progress had been made toward establishing a carpet industry during those latter years of the Stuart Period, little or no progress had been made in the development of design. Most factories were turning out copies of Oriental rugs. Small hand-knotting establishments created special designs to order—many bearing crests, shields, or coats of arms. A few rugs, like tapestries, were allegorical, some illustrating early feats, jousts, biblical stories, or landscapes of the happy farm life. These knotted or embroidered pictorial carpets were actually called table carpets and under no circumstances were they used on the floor. For pleasure, ladies also contributed to the family decor by embroidering small rugs almost always floral in character.

The Early Georgian Period (1714–1760), a time of peaceful prosperity, brought a sense of independence and ebullience to the English people. The Grand Tour, a prerequisite to the education of all well-bred young people, encouraged the re-evaluation of classic architecture in Greece, in France, and especially in Italy, where the contemporary Baroque style could also be viewed. By the turn of the century many English landowners had hired Italian architects versed in the Grand Baroque Style to build into the sweeping English countryside houses that were large and florid. It was surely The Age of Elegance, if not of doubtful taste. It was not until the 1720's that reason distilled a more refined and disciplined style of architecture, the Palladian Style, a wholly British expression, at variance with those excesses of the turn of the century and of the French Baroque styles of Louis XV and Louis XVI. The British refinements closely followed the dictates of *Vitruvius Britannicus*, a book written by the scholarly and greatly admired architect, Colin Campbell.

This so-called Age of Elegance saw a greatly expanded city of London, whose population had grown to over one-half a million citizens, making it the largest city within the country. And as such, London maintained a very urban character of its own. Inigo Jones almost a century earlier had shown the way to design town houses as part of the coherent architectural city scheme; and London had been virtually rebuilt after the great fire, following many of his principles. The great new dome of St. Paul's, rebuilt by Sir Christopher Wren, looked down over a growing leisure class and developing international society. Fashionable men rose late—around three in the afternoon—and spent the evening until the early hours of the morning at clubs playing cards, at the theatre, or at receptions. The women spent their days, when not at embroidery, in much the same manner. The Society of the Dilettanti was organized in 1733 to promote the arts. The members held an enormous influence over the public's taste in architecture and decoration. Literary figures of the time included Ben Johnson, Pope, Fielding, Richardson, Defoe, and Swift.

Overriding all intellectual and social pursuits was one development of great importance for the future of the country. A method of using coke to smelt iron was developed by the Darbys of Coalbrooke. The method paved the way to the growth of the great coal fields of middle England and to the eventual industrialization of the vast iron and steel industries.

Demands were being made on the textile industry to improve their products and to develop design suitable for the more sophisticated market within the country, the colonies, and the many and growing number of tropical markets. Dyeing and finishing were improved. But it was the Royal Society of Arts that was responsible for raising the design standard of the carpet industry, a standard which brought a needed focus of attention to the industry.

In 1756 the Society, in an effort to entice artists to submit designs of some quality for the craftsmen to weave, set aside a premium of £150 as an award to be given annually in controlled competition. The first two craftsmen engaged in weaving to receive a share of the award were Thomas Moore of the Chriswell Street, Mooresfield factory, and Thomas Whitty of Axminster. Whitty later won two other awards. (More than twenty years later the results of this award program were recorded in the first volume of the Society's "Transactions" (1783) ". . . it [the award program] is now established in different parts of the Kingdom and brought [the design and weave] to a degree of beauty which 'Turkey' [imported] carpets never attained."

Thomas Whitty, a simple weaver at Axminster, had the good fortune to see in the home of a friend several fine examples of imported Turkish carpets. These so impressed him that he attempted to weave one for himself on his standard horizontal fabric loom. The solution completely eluded him, and with much difficulty he succeeded in weaving only a small piece. Whitty later made an incognito trip to a rival factory, one successfully using vertical looms, and run by a French *immigré*, Peter Parisot, a Huguenot. Parisot, having fled the intolerable working conditions at the Royal Savonnerie factory in Paris, had managed in 1751 to solicit the patronage of the Duke of Cumberland and set up a factory in Paddington. (The first carpets from this establishment were commissioned by the Duke as a gift for the Prince of Wales.) Here Whitty learned the elusive technique of weaving a Turkey carpet.

On his return to Axminster, Whitty had a large upright loom built and trained his daughters to weave in the Turkish manner. This was the start of a factory operation which existed for almost a century. (His first Royal Society award was won after only twelve months of operations.)

Mrs. Abigail Adams, wife of the American minister to England, and future mistress of the White House, visited Whitty's factory on September 15, 1778, and wrote to her sister,

It [Axminster] is a small place, but has two manufacturers of note; one of carpets, and one of tapes; both of which we visited. The manufactory of the carpets is wholly performed by women and children. You would have been surprised to see in how ordinary a building this rich manufactory is carried on. A few glass windows in some of our barns would be equal to it. They have but two prices for their carpets woven here; the one is eighteen shillings, and the other twenty-four, a square yard. They are woven of any dimension you please, and without a seam. The colors are beautiful, and the carpets are very durable.

Later in her own diary she noted, "The carpets are equally durable with the Turkey, but surpass them in colours and figure."

Competition was growing keen, and shortly after Whitty started his Axminster operation, a second Huguenot, Passavant, started a factory at the wool center at Exeter. Some few years later, Passavant heard that his fellow countryman, Parisot was in some financial trouble. He offered to buy the equipment of the Paddington factory and set it up at Exeter.

The following year Thomas Moore, a second winner of a Royal Society award, opened his factory at Mooresfield within the City of London. There he manufactured hand-woven tapestries and hand-knotted rugs.

Examples of the work of Moore, Whitty, and Passavant all reflect the fashion of the mid-eighteenth century. There were ebullient florals and designs of Greco-Roman classical persuasion. All three factories reproduced Oriental carpets, emulating both pattern and knotting. Early in 1768, Lady Mary Coke visited the factory at Mooresfield and reported "several different kinds" of carpets of (undoubtedly) designs of Thomas Moore, and "there are other kinds that are made like the persian, look quite well." A similar observation was made in 1777 by Samuel Curwen while visiting Thomas Whitty's factory at Axminster ". . . here is also wrought besides his own, of a peculiar construction, Turkey carpets, so very like in figure, colour, and thickness, as not to be distinguished from the genuine article."

Moore's own designs, however, were the embodiment of the neo-classical style. His designs, so obviously dictated by Robert Adam, indicated a certain precise arrangement of circular and octagonal *paterae*, bell flower swags, wreaths, anthemions, Greek keys, and *guilloche* borders.

On the other hand, those of Passavant signed and dated during the late

1750's, were also elaborate. They appeared somewhat ponderous, bowed down as they were with Rococo scrolls, foliated motifs, and flowers. Original carpets emanating from Axminster were more delicate, with medallions, ribbons, floral bouquets, baskets, and garlands arranged in a restrained manner, indicating a refined Greco-Roman tradition.

About 1740, under the auspices of Lord Pembroke, the manufacture of Brussels carpets was introduced at Wilton. These carpets had loop piles, not unlike a terry cloth. A knifing action was devised, which cut the loops to give the pile a velvet texture not unlike the present day velvets still manufactured at Wilton.

One outstanding example of a mid-eighteenth century English hand-woven carpet is the one made for Mount Vernon, home of George Washington. This had a tree pattern reminiscent of needle embroidery. For convenience, it was made in two pieces later joined together. The weavers' signatures in bold letters read "ANN NEVILLE AND PARNELL NEVILLE 1746."

In spite of all this activity, carpets were still being imported from Persia and Turkey. Canterbury Cathedral lists several in its inventory of 1735 ". . . a Persian carpet and a Turkey carpet . . . a very large new Turkey carpet and two small carpets."

Designs for domestic rugs made by the ladies of the house during the Early Georgian days were, as always, hand-embroidered floral patterns.

Great industrial changes began to take place during the Late Georgian Period (1760–1810). In 1764 the spinning jenny was invented by Arkwright, thereby hastening the tedious process of the uniform spinning of yarns and cutting the high cost of labor considerably. In the same year, Watt invented the steam engine, paving the way for other mechanically driven steam engines—cylinder printing of textiles (1783), and finally the power loom (1785). For the first time manufacturing was seriously able to compete with agriculture as a leading industry of England.

During this same period textile patterns played a less dominant role in the household interior. That is not to say that the use of carpets diminished, but the taste of the age tended more toward plain, single-colored, unpatterned carpets, possibly as a result of the style limitations of the new power looms. Patterns of the other textiles (upholstery and drapery) in the room had discreet polychrome colors. The artist-decorator set the pace for interior design, and the use of quiet, somber colors and patterns allowed a subtlety of arrangement of line and form. Where patterns did exist on carpets, they tended to echo the intricate plasterwork of the ceiling.

Probably one of the most famous exponents of the severe classical style were the brothers Adam. John, the elder, and Robert held a dictatorial sway over a segment of English nobility by demanding not only full autonomy over the architectural form of the building, outside and in, but in furnishings which were designed to relate in scale and ornamentation. Despite this, the Adams were the most lionized of all architect-decorators of the time.

The Adams designed many of the hand-woven carpets made at a number of factories—all commissions for houses under renovation or construction. One famous Adam carpet made at Mooresfield is still in use at Syon House, seat of the Duke of Northumberland; others are at Osterley Park, seat of the Earl of Jersey.

In 1790 Whitty wove by hand a large carpet for the Throne Room at Carlton House, and another grand carpet for that Oriental fantasy, the Pavilion at Brighton. Ironically enough, Whitty was also commissioned by the Sultan of Turkey, the head of a country which undoubtedly had produced the largest number of export carpets for England.

Despite the fact that a few factories were turning to power-driven looms for faster, less expensive production, many of the revered factories that still specialized in the very fine quality hand-knotted or tapestry weave carpets continued to produce many carpets on commission for the rich. The Prince Regent alone spent some £160,000 within a three-year period on his furnishings, which included many fine carpets. John Nash, an architect of the Regency Period, had already begun the building of some of the famous terraces and villas of Regent's Park and other private houses. The late days of the Georgian era were one of vast prosperity.

Although many Aubussons were being imported from France, Kidderminster in 1807 maintained a factory of over a thousand hand looms at work producing carpets. Designs, under the influence of the Adams, had become classical in feeling with a few emulating the Pompeiian style. Floral motifs were enclosed by large central architectural motifs and narrow rectangular or attenuated diamonds at either end.

Following on the heels of the Late Georgian Period came the Regency (1810–1830). This was a stylistic period greatly influenced by the taste and classic revivalism of Napoleon. The neighborhoods of Brighton, Cheltenham, and Regent's Park, with houses set in terraces and squares, were not only the focus of chic society but set a new decorative trend.

Striped upholstery and drapery fabrics were very popular. This was also a period of Oriental revival, and Chippendale, the current cabinetmaker, developed his own fantasies in the *chinois* style with cut-out and figured patterns on chairs, *étagères*, mirror frames, etc. Carpet patterns emulated the Chinese rage and sprouted patterns of dragons and coiled serpents. Two fragments of hand-knotted Axminster carpets, all that was left of the large number of carpets woven for the Pavilion at Brighton, show a mixture of Oriental and floral motifs. The music room carpet, purely Chinese in design, showed a pair of dragons and sacred symbols in shades of gold on a blue ground. A similar carpet, woven for the banquet hall, bore a central motif of a dragon coiled with three serpents. These were surrounded with diversely wrought circles, increasing in diameter toward the border edges.

The active days at Axminster were on the wane, and in order to fill the important Pavilion order, barely a hundred women were employed on less than twenty looms. The carpets were still of the highest hand-woven quality, thick and luxurious, made of top-grade wools dyed with fine dyes. But for Axminster, these were virtually the last of the significant commissions, and in 1835 the factory was forced to close its doors.

England of the mid-century was over-extended around the world, supporting its vast colonial empire, and while there was certain export advantage, the population of England and Wales combined did not exceed ten million people. All were financially pressed in protecting their outposts. The harassment of Napoleon with wars in Egypt (1798) and later, the naval blockade of the British merchant fleet in 1803, followed in 1818 by a further embarrassment, the threat by the United States of a blockade, had all placed a severe strain on the country's resources. The rich were feeling the pinch.

The harnessing of two natural resources, steam and electricity, led to a quick development in the power-driven machine, which in turn began to replace generations of handcraft work in factories. The machine turned out a large quantity of products faster and certainly cheaper for a mass of people who wanted furnishings that were attractive and comfortable at a price they could afford.

Industrial England of the mid-nineteenth century was again riding the crest of the wave. Steam and electricity brought with them not only a faster, cheaper, method of production, but the railroad to carry raw materials to factories and finished goods to market.

Machines enabled carpets and rugs to be well within the budget of the average household and the industry flourished. Every apartment and house was carpeted. The main industry was located in Kidderminster, Halifax, Yorkshire, Wilton, Axminster, and Bridgenorth; and in Edinburgh and Kilmarnock, Scotland. Many of these were former centers of handwoven carpets. By 1850 there were over four thousand looms working at Kidderminster alone.

The simplest type carpet produced was "venetian," a check or stripe pattern, with a wool face over a cotton or hemp warp. The narrowness and tight weave of the venetian made it ideal for a stair runner or it could be pieced together for wall-to-wall carpeting. The double-face or two-cloth type was still in vogue, and by 1850 an exuberant pattern of Chinese motifs, superimposed on a plaid ground, was particularly popular. Florals had Renaissance jewel forms at intersections of the design and there was a general confusion of naturalistic and stylistic forms.

In 1832 Richard Wytock of Edinburgh patented his invention for a tapestry type. This was followed in 1839 by John Templeton of Glasgow who patented an Axminster chenille-type carpet weave. The Patented Tapestry had a preprinted warp while the Patented Axminster had a basic chenille weave, with a second, or extra, color warp to bind the chenille. One Patented Axminster was made in three main panels with ornamented bands and garlands of flowers. The panel ground was covered with a damask-like pattern. In the center was a large cartouche, bearing the date 1850 in Roman numerals. These three types of complex weaves enabled machine-made carpets to emulate more closely the intricacies of hand-knotted carpets.

After the two patented weaves became available to other mills, a number of factories produced carpets with Gothic millefleurs designs. By 1840 large Louis XV Rococo scrolls were refined to appear more architectural and symmetrical. While the nation was enthusiastic over the enormous possibilities of steam power machines, the Prince Consort, measuring the public's optimism, announced a Great Exhibition of the Works of Industry—an exhibition which would symbolize England's place as "Workshop of the World." It was to be a monster production, one which would far outdistance in scope and scale all previous European exhibitions.

To house it, Sir Joseph Paxton designed a gigantic structure of glass and iron to be built in Hyde Park. It was to be twice the width, and four times the length of St. Paul's Cathedral.

Sir Joseph's "Crystal Palace" formed a giant conservatory around a whole grove of elm trees and its four hundred tons of glass was supported by 3,230 colums. Disraeli described it as "an enchanted pile . . . raised to the

glory of England and the delight of two hemispheres." The cost was
£176,030. There were twenty-one acres of galleries and halls in which to
display both machinery and products. There were over six million visitors.

Although a few of the carpet trade had been slow to put in power-
driven looms prior to the exhibition, twenty-two manufacturers did exhibit.
One, John Crossley & Sons of Halifax, exhibited twelve different designs in
tapestry, velvet, and tapestry Brussels, and several mosaic designs, the most
interesting of which were four medallion designs, each made in two sections.
Another exhibitor was the American, Erastus Bigelow, who displayed his
power loom—the first capable of weaving Brussels carpets. It was Bigelow,
who twelve years earlier, had invented the first power loom for making
double ingrain, or Kidderminster carpet. This loom was also on exhibition
and was immediately purchased by Scottish and English manufacturers who
attended the exhibition. But the Brussels-type loom remained unsold. Eventually the Crossleys bought it for £10,000.

The previous spring, Francis Crossley, one of the founder's three sons,
had invited a Yorkshire man named Collier to Crossley's Dean Clough Mill
in Halifax. Collier's success with his power looms had attracted Crossley's
attention and once there, Collier produced a model loom incorporating a
special feature, a wire motion. When Collier received the Bigelow Brussels
loom, he combined the best of his own with the new one with such great
success that all carpet manufacturers in the country were forced to adopt
Collier's loom or cease production.

The great Crystal Palace exhibition served one other great function; it
pointed up the need for some relationship between the artist-designer and
manufacturer. In spite of the great advances of machine production, with
the exception of a few "art manufacturers" whose products were designed
to be esthetically pleasing, there was little artistic achievement in most products presented.

Regarding the many styles that abounded at the time, an early Victorian
journal dated 1849, *Hints for Decoration and Furnishings of Dwellings*,
gives a glimpse of this period of eclectic confusion of styles

. . . There is no general agreement of principle and taste. Everyone elects his
own style of art . . . some few have taken refuge in a liking of pure Greek and
are highly classical; others find safety in the antique; others believe in Pugin;
others lean upon imitations of modern Germans; and some extol Renaissance. We
all agree only in being imitators.

Even with the dizzying number of styles, color, and arrangement of pattern, the scale was quite original. The Victorian equation of elaboration was exemplified by the use of pattern on all available surfaces. The carefully balanced color schemes of the classic, and in particular, the Adam decorative scheme, were too refined. Colors during the period 1850–1880 were dark crimson, bottle green, and black—a scheme meant to give a rich effect.

While the English were applauding products made on power-driven machines, a group of dissidents were rebelling against an esthetic stagnation brought on by an emphasis on machine technology. Under the leadership of architect John Ruskin, his disciple, William Morris, and members of a group called the "Pre-Raphaelites," led by Rosetti, they strove to find a means to re-unite art with technology. Morris was himself a superb craftsman, designing at the time not only the finest wallpapers, fabrics, and furniture, but also later the design and weave of rugs and carpets—a more complicated but satisfying medium. The concern of this group, later called "The Arts and Crafts Movement," which, in its more general terms, spread throughout Europe, was that

a work of art—be it hand or machine made—should be an expression of man's delight in his labor, a joy to its maker, as well as to the user under a condition of social equality—it must be for all. For without these conditions, art would fall, a victim to the heartless process of mechanization.

To clarify his own philosophy, Morris explained that function related always to human life and activity, not only to the object. It was his plan to establish an association of reputable artists who would devote their talents toward the design and making of better furnishings on a craft basis. Morris, as a working designer, and Morris the philosopher, part of a movement in revolt, became, as Gropius once said, "a spiritual ancestor of the Bauhaus." He explored ancient craft techniques, and fought to preserve hand-made imperfections. Embroidery had always been an important interest, but the dyestuffs available were unreliable. He turned to dyeing. In 1876 he learned silk weaving, not just the mechanics, but the important step of translating his designs by literally "painting" his patterns on finely squared graph paper to indicate each interweave or crossing of the warp and weft threads. This important step he tried to adapt to the design of mechanically woven carpets. His first carpet design for Kidderminster was a disaster. He had not realized the difference between the mechanical weave and the hand loom.

In April 1878, Morris bought a new home with a small coach house attached. He filled this small building with Hammersmith carpet looms and began to weave (the operation was later moved to Merton). For him it was a satisfying creative expression.

Morris was an interpreter of designs in the Art Nouveau style, harking back to the naturalistic flowers and reinterpreting them in a fluid, artistic manner. His studies for carpet weave were mainly with Orientals, "they show us the way to set about designing such things . . ." (and of modern carpets) ". . . while they by no means should imitate them in design but show themselves obviously to be the outcome of modern and western ideas."

The result of Morris' efforts, though by no means prolific, was noble. One large carpet for the Earl of Carlisle's drawing room at Naworth was finished in 1881. It took nearly a year to complete by hand and it weighed "a ton." A second impressive carpet was hand made for the Earl of Portsmouth. This was an arc-shaped carpet made to fit a room at Hurstbourne, and had a floral pattern interrupted by three large shields bearing the arms of the Earl and the Countess of Portsmouth.

In 1884, Morris was instrumental in setting up the Arts and Crafts Exhibition Society, and in 1886 he finally interested the government into investigating the training of artists and designers for machine production. The school was established in 1887 for the education of what today are termed students of industrial design.

By the end of the nineteenth century, machines had been developed which could weave an almost unlimited variety of carpets. Many mills specialized in certain weaves and others with a broad spectrum. Patterns, both in repeats, or non-repeats, of a symmetrical or asymmetrical scheme, florals, plaids, and plain cloth appeared. The names of the early hand-weave factories have today become generic terms; other names have evolved also from the hand-weaves.

Brussels: These carpets are characterized by a pile surface similar to the low pile surface of a velvet fabric or an Oriental carpet. The weave is believed to have been developed in 1740 at Wilton and Kidderminster. The pattern was created by using differently colored threads for the pile and bringing them to the surface whenever a particular color was called for in the design.

Ingrain: Sometimes known as Scotch, Kilmarnock carpets, Kidderminster, or English. These are a pileless loom-woven floorcovering of double construction, not unlike the two-ply coverlets for beds. Two cloths of different colors are woven and interwoven in such a manner that the yarns of the first, or top cloth, appear on the surface then yarns of the second, or under cloth, are brought to the surface. This created a smooth-face or flat material, with designs of both colors appearing on both sides. "Ingrain" was perhaps the most correct terminology for this type weave, for the yarns were literally ingrained into each other. During the eighteenth century ingrain carpets were woven on 36-inch wide looms and for larger carpets, strips were sewn together.

Wilton: This is a cut-pile carpet (a Brussels type with the surface loops cut with a knifing action during the weaving process). Wiltons were often patterned with floral or geometric designs, woven in the same manner as Brussels. This carpeting too was woven in narrow (28- or 26-inch) strips joined to make a wider carpet.

Axminster: Like Wilton, the word Axminster denotes both a place and a type of carpet weave. In contrast to the looped and cut-pile floorcoverings that were woven in narrow widths, Axminsters could be woven in room-size widths without seaming. The pile, instead of being woven as an integral part of the foundation, was knotted to the warp threads which formed the foundation similar to that of the Oriental Ghiordes knotting process. This knotting by machinery was developed and used by Peter Parisot when he started his manufactory in the eighteenth century at Fulham, and was later adopted by Thomas Whitty at Axminster after his visit to the Fulton factory in 1754.

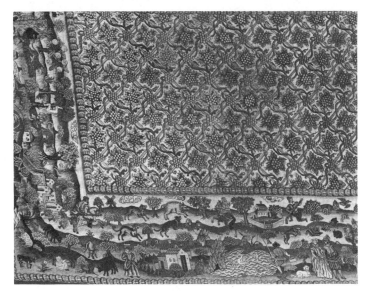

English. Elizabethan needlework. *Courtesy of Perez Ltd., London.*

English, late 16th century. Linen embroidered with colored silk in tent stitch. Table carpet (detail). *Victoria and Albert Museum.*

English. Border detail of "Lucretia's Banquet,"
wool and silk on canvas in tent stitch. *Victoria
and Albert Museum.*

English, late 16th cen-
tury. Linen embroi-
dered with colored silk
in tent stitch. Table
carpet (detail). *Victo-
ria and Albert Museum.*

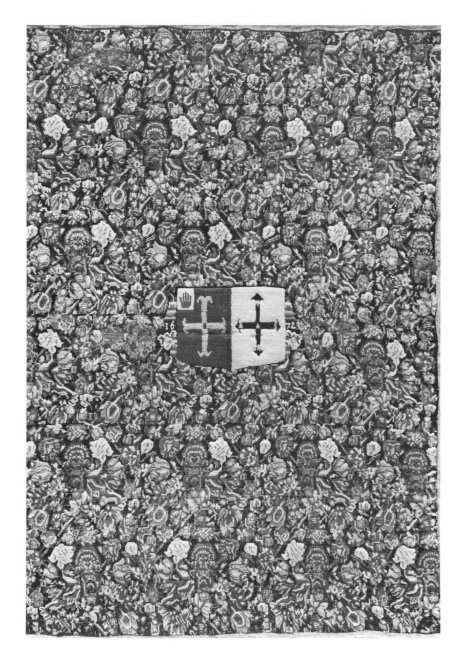

English, 1672. Knotted wool pile. *Victoria and Albert Museum.*

Opposite page: English, early 17th century. Needlework carpet. *Victoria and Albert Museum.*

English, first half 18th century. Embroidered in colored wool on linen. *Victoria and Albert Museum.*

English, 1743. Wool embroidered on canvas. Initials probably "E. W." *The Metropolitan Museum of Art, Gift of Irwin Untermyer, 1962.*

English, second quarter 18th century. Embroidered in wool on canvas. *Victoria and Albert Museum.*

English, 1757. Wool pile carpet. Made at Exeter. *Victoria and Albert Museum.*

English, circa 1780. Rare George III. Mooresfield carpet designed by Adam. *Courtesy of Parke-Bernet Galleries.*

English, 1765. Wool embroidered on canvas. *The Metropolitan Museum of Art, Pulitzer Bequest, 1934.*

English, mid-18th century. Knotted pile. Robert Adam design for Osterley Park House. Executed by Thomas Moore. *Victoria and Albert Museum.*

English, 1765. Rare George III needlepoint. *Courtesy of Parke-Bernet Galleries.*

116

English. Wool pile carpet. 18th–19th century. Axminster in the Adam style. *Victoria and Albert Museum.*

English, 1790. Needlepoint. George III. *Courtesy of Parke-Bernet Galleries, Berberyan Collection.*

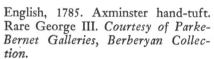

English, 1785. Axminster hand-tuft. Rare George III. *Courtesy of Parke-Bernet Galleries, Berberyan Collection.*

English, 1780–90. Wool. Probably an Axminster design after Adam style. *The Metropolitan Museum of Art.*

English, circa 1790. Important George III Axminster medallion carpet. *Courtesy of Parke-Bernet Galleries, Berberyan Collection.*

English, needlework map. Signed Ann Wilkinson, March 7, 1810. *Courtesy of Perez, Ltd., London.*

English, circa 1820. Hand tufted flora. George IV. *Courtesy of Parke-Bernet Galleries, Berberyan Collection.*

English, circa 1825. Needlepoint. George IV. *Courtesy of Parke-Bernet Galleries.*

English, circa 1830. Needlework. Important George IV. *Courtesy of Parke-Bernet Galleries, Berberyan Collection.*

English, 1843. Early Victorian needlework. *Courtesy of Perez, Ltd., London.*

English, first half 19th century. Chenille Axminster. Maker unknown but probably James Templeton of Glasgow, the inventor of this process of weaving. Described in Sotheby's catalog as having been ordered the first half of the 19th century for the drawing room of 44 Berkley Square, London. Manufactured prior to the steam power loom. Now in possession of the Ditchley Foundation.

English, circa 1845. Needlepoint. Important Victorian carpet. *Courtesy of Parke-Bernet Galleries, Berberyan Collection.*

English, first half 19th century. Thick wool pile on flax warp Axminster. *Victoria and Albert Museum.*

English, mid-19th century. Knotted wool pile. *Victoria and Albert Museum.*

English, needlepoint, probably Victorian. *Courtesy of Parke-Bernet Galleries, Berberyan Collection.*

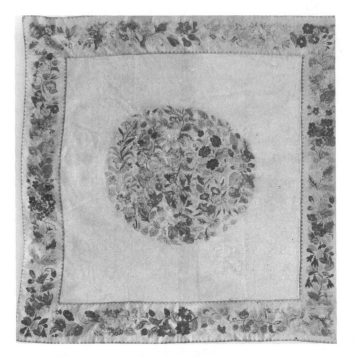

English, mid-19th century. Wool embroidered on linen. *The Metropolitan Museum of Art, Gift of Mrs. J. V. McMullan, 1959.*

English, 1851. Worsted pointed in two sections. *Courtesy of John Crossley & Sons, England.*

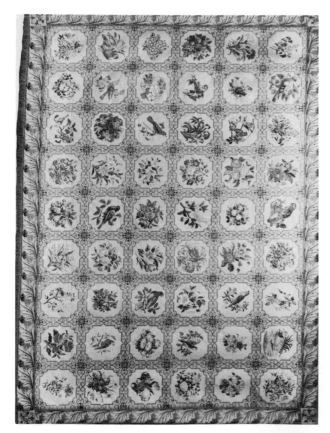

English, circa 1855. Victorian needlework. *Courtesy of Perez, Ltd., London.*

English, 1860. Worsted printed body (detail). *Courtesy of John Crossley & Sons, England.*

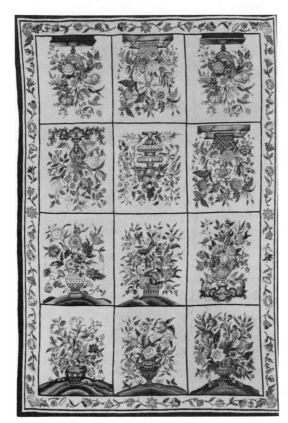

Left: English, mid-20th century. Floral needlepoint faithfully reproduced from original made by H. M. Queen Mary. *Courtesy of Parke-Bernet Galleries.*

Right: English, late 19th century, silk. Made by William Morris at Merton Abbey. *Courtesy of Perez, Ltd., London.*

Opposite page: English. Knotted in woolen pile on cotton warp. Butterswood carpet designed by William Morris. *Victoria and Albert Museum.*

English, 1906, printed carpet showing "Pharaoh's daughter in procession down the Nile after finding Moses." Manufactured for the Balkan States, particularly Rumania. This carpet would have been hung on the wall. *Courtesy of John Crossley & Sons, England.*

English, carpet designed by Adam. Adam architecture. The Gallery of Landsdowne House, City of Westminster, London. *Courtesy of National Monument Record.*

English, about 1810. Probably an Axminster, hand tufted. Banqueting Room, Royal Pavilion, Brighton. Original carpet made for the room was an Axminster designed by Robert Jones. Style was pseudo-Chinese with a pattern of central circular motif enclosing a dragon with three serpents curled around it and involving it. These are surrounded with a series of circles diversely wrought and increasing in diameter toward the border. It no longer exists. This carpet is an acquisition for the restoration.

English, mid-19th century. Chenille carpet. *Victoria and Albert Museum.*

SCANDINAVIA

4

THE IMPORTANT HANDICRAFTS of the Scandinavian countries, weaving and embroidery, were the two crafts which, like the sagas and folklore, were handed down from mother to daughter for many generations dating as far back as the Bronze Age. Life in these northern lands was austere, and for centuries people were occupied with their own small, isolated world, little influenced by the more sophisticated cultures of the other European countries. Because of this cultural isolation, the patterns women wove into their rya rugs, though not primitive, are delightfully naive and refreshing. These patterns were a true creative expression of the weaver, limited only by the lack of dyes available to them.

Historically, Sweden existed as early as A.D. 98 as a "mighty" nation of shipbuilders, ruled from Uppsala by the Ynglings. But as an empire, according to Nestor's Chronicles, it only came into being in 862 under the leadership of Rurik and his brothers, Sineus and Trevor. The inhabitants were referred to as "*rus*" or "*ross*" (probably derived from the region which was, and still is, called Roslagen, in the district of East Uppland). Historians have been led to believe that the word "Russian" also evolved from this same root word and, in fact, the Swedish people did maintain large colonies in territories 133 that are now within Russian borders. These colonies acted as garrisons from which the Swedes were able to control the people farther north—the Finns and Slavs. The Swedes also did a brisk fur trapping business from these northern outposts, in which they bartered for precious metals, silks, spices, and other luxuries in the outer or eastern sections of Russia and the Orient. The success of these trading ventures and the protection of the trade routes later precipitated the many Viking raids.

During the tenth century, the Swedes became increasingly assimilated with the Slavs. The population, for instance, in Kiev a few years later (in 1018) consisted mainly of people of Swedish background called, interestingly enough, "*daner*." About the same time several groups whose ancestors had been those early ruling Ynglings, divided up. "Harald the Fair" established a kingdom in what is now called Norway; and the royal family of the Skjoldungs established a similar kingdom, which became Denmark.

Until the time of the Viking raids—about the end of the 9th century—all these northern peoples spoke one language, dialects which eventually evolved into the distinct languages of Swedish, Danish, and Norwegian.

Until 1809, Suomi (Finland) was a province of Sweden, protecting the mother country from Russian border raids, and as such, that small country saw much strife, belonging first to one and then the other throughout her long history. Unlike the pure blooded northern people of the other Scandinavian countries, the Finnish ancestry was of mixed races, having been overrun in early times by nomadic tribes from Hungary; and although her natural cultural ties were with Sweden, there is always a small but noticeable tinge of the exotic to be found in Finland's language, peasant arts, and folklore, which can only be explained by this outside, southern "drop of blood."

Rya Rugs

The early ryas were bedspreads, usually made for the young bride's trousseau; sometimes the young couple stood on their ryas during the ceremony, later sleeping under them on their wedding night. Ryas were also used as sleigh covers, and at times to warm the horses. Sometimes a beautiful rya was hung on the wall, but whatever the circumstance, these ryas were an important part of the family heritage, passed down from mother to daughter. There was a certain status granted those who owned many and beautiful rya rugs.

The earliest ryas were somber in color, for it was not until the fifteenth or sixteenth centuries that the colors became lighter and brighter. In those early days the young couple were not able to own their home, and until they became established, they often slept in a lean-to or ante-room of the parents' house where the floor or cot had to make do. The rugs they slept under were of necessity utilitarian, made not to show dirt.

The word *rya* is from the old Scandinavian *ry* (the plural, *ryor*) meaning rough and shaggy pile, and one would guess that those early ryas were not unlike fur with long, shaggy, natural wool piles. The rya, or *flossa*, weave alternates a knotted pile with a tapestry weave. Whereas the Oriental carpet generally has one or two woven wefts between each row of knotted pile, the rya differs both in the number of woven rows—generally varying from eight to ten—and in the length of the pile. Some have been found with as many as twenty rows of tapestry weave intervening between the knotted pile rows.

There are also numerous varieties of weaves within the *ryor* group. One, the *glossa*, with a knot similar to the Oriental or Ghiordes knot, is believed to be an independent solution developed in the northern countries and not a copy of the Oriental knot at all. Another weave, the *lassna*, from the Swedish word *lasa*, has a somewhat primitive Jacquard type solution whereby warp threads are picked up by hand to form the pattern. Both low-warp (horizontal looms), and high-warp (vertical looms) have been known to be used. In Sweden the low-warp weaves were called *rollakan*, a derivation of the Swedish word meaning wallcovering or chair throw. The high-warp, low-pile weave, using a standard type tapestry weave, was called *flamskvavnad*, or Flemish weave.

The rya was undoubtedly the most significant, certainly the most expressive, of all the folk arts—particularly during the seventeenth and eighteenth centuries when beautiful colors and patterns were used. It is generally conceded, however, that the most beautiful ryas come from Finland, with the largest proportion of those coming from the southern and western sections.

In Sweden, ryas could be found in Norrland and Skåne to the south, but these do not have the artistic purity and value of the Finnish ryas. Their originality did not relate as personally to the country's folklore or tradition but instead showed decided influences from outside countries. That ryas were used in Sweden was evident from a number of inventories found over the ages—one such inventory having been found in the cloisters at Vadstena, a section of Sweden belonging at one time to Denmark. Others, dated 1506, were in inventories found in the castle at Stegeholm which mention that guest beds were covered with ryas. In 1522, the Swedish author, Peter Hansson, wrote in his book on military tactics that ". . . in case there is a hole in the stone wall (protecting the camp), rya rugs are to be used to fill them. They are so strong they make an excellent stuffing." This would indicate that there must have been a large number of ryas woven for issue to the army, although to anyone's knowledge, none have survived.

Those early rya rugs from Norway remained even more primitive, having neither color nor interesting patterns. Evidently those too were of more utilitarian nature rather than artistic. It is known that early Norwegian real estate transactions between the years 1400 and 1480 used rya rugs in barter for land.

No early rya rugs can be traced to Denmark, although a similar weave was found to produce pillows and other small items, with subtle colors and little pattern. Evidently this art, too, died out many years ago.

In all three countries, Sweden, Norway, and Denmark, the noble families used imported fabrics from more exotic countries near or around the Mediterranean. Peasants wove their more utilitarian fabrics. This was not so in Finland, where ladies of good families wove many of the beautiful rugs—some of which are still in private collections today. As in England, the act of weaving was considered one of the great artistic expressions of the country. It is interesting to note that all the handwoven rya rugs remained of bedcover size even long after they had been accepted for use as rugs for the floor. By 1560–1570, the making and use of ryas was very common, and by the year 1620, the practice had almost all but disappeared. This was, however, only a temporary dearth brought on by the practice of landowners who took to collecting the rugs in lieu of taxes and even to grant title to the land.

As mentioned above, the early ryas were shaggy or furry looking, but as time went on the pile became flatter and designs became more intricate. As looms were narrow, two long rugs were sewn together. The strip where they were joined was called *listas*. At times these *listas* were in a color other than the main field of the two lengths to be joined.

The earliest Finnish inventories scrupulously described much of the color in the rugs, but unfortunately nothing of the patterns themselves. This possibly is an indication that their rugs were of plain, solid colors. Later, simple geometrics were added for interest; and still later, patterns became more intricate.

Early colors were white, black, and gray (natural wool colors). Occasionally, yellow began to appear as did red—both colors available from dyes found in local plants or berries. Complex colors, such as blue or green, were rarely used, as plants did not produce them and commercial dyes were not available.

When geometric patterns first appeared, the most common color combinations were black and white; gray and black; or white, red and black with yellow.

In general, however, it seems the less decorative rya rugs were to be found in the southeastern sections of Finland. The further west one traveled, the more colorful and decorative the designs. Each area had its own traditional patterns and color combinations. In the 1558 inventories found at Uppland castle, white ryas with black striped borders were mentioned. Another inventory of the same date in Helsinki, speaks of yellow borders. Both groups of rya rugs were woven for local ruling families—heads of "duchies," as each territory was called.

As weavers became more adventurous, patterns developed elongated "leaves," small rectangles, or discs of color, dotted about the surface of the plain color field. These geometric forms varied in size within the same rug.

The first coat of arms to make its appearance seems to have been around 1559, when it was used as the important motif on a rug woven for Kastelhölm Castle, a duchy located on the Gulf of Bothnia. A second appeared the following year and was listed in the inventory of Turku Castle.

Most of the fine rya rugs for these castles were woven by the wives of the nobles or heads of the duchy, but in many cases local artisans were hired from the village to do the weaving.

During the seventeenth century rya rugs turned up in many an inventory of parish priests, and there seem to have been two types listed—a single weave, and a reverse weave. Unfortunately, no mention was made as to the pattern. This did not necessarily mean that patterns did not exist, but rather that inventories neglected to inform us.

Finnish ryas dating from the turn of the seventeenth century to the mid-nineteenth century still exist in both private and museum collections. They are highly prized as collectors' items, both for the beauty of pattern and for the clarity of color. Many were woven by professional weavers who traveled in teams of two around the countryside. They carried portable looms which they set up in private homes. One did the knotting, but both were needed to lift the heavy harness. During this period the most common warp was flax, cotton, or hemp. The pile was wool. The weave was a tapestry weave not unlike that of the Gobelin tapestry. Compositions were geometric in character which later led to the more sophisticated diamonds, and crosses set into large, plain color fields.

In the northern and eastern regions of Finland, each rug pattern was apparently a free expression of its designer. There seemed to be no adherence to any strict local folk art or custom. Rugs tended to be primitive, even childish in character, and color was the important element. In the central sections of Finland, quite the contrary; beautiful rya rugs were found. Designs were rather special, with a diversified composition and color. There one found yellow, blue, brown, a natural wool color, and black. Squares, irregular squares, and the traditional "wheel" pattern—a quatrefoil design centered within a diamond outline. This was particular to the Duchy of Häme. The design seems to have had a middle European origin. All Finnish crafts support a smattering of middle European or Byzantine character, stemming from its early antecedents. It is, however, interesting to note that no Slavic or Russian style ever pervaded any of the Finnish folk arts. Rya rugs found in the central areas of Finland, dating from 1772, appeared to have figures of men and women, and those dating from 1773, the form of a heart. The placement of these motifs and the geometric patterns was often asymmetrical rather than balanced.

The traditional Finnish symbol, Hannunvakuuna—the coat of arms of Hans—was taken from the great epic *Karevala*, a series of legendary poems. One of the epic's great heroes around whom the poems evolved was a man named Hans. This symbol appeared in almost all forms of Finnish folk art and the symbol was considered a harbinger of good luck, warding off evil spirits. The symbol resembles a square with an outcropping of circular corners. In the more primitive weaves where the soft curved line was difficult to weave, this symbol appears to have small squares as extensions at each of the four corners of the larger central square.

Patterns in the western sections of the country remained the most static over the years, adhering to a strict set of traditional forms: figures of men and women, trees and birds, squares or dice. The tree—a religious symbol—represented good and evil. The symbolism was closely linked to the Adam and Eve mystique of original sin. The Christian religion pervaded the areas of Satakunta and Rauma first. Here also were found the "ring knot" or "link knot" ryas (at Satakunta), and the single tree or tree of life pattern (Rauma). Slightly east, the trees (single, two, or three to a rug) take on a more sophisticated appearance, developing into a virtual forest. In the Tampere area, trees became mixed with other design elements. In most cases the tree patterns bearing stiff straight branches predated those with the more graceful bent branches. The latter show a distinct Norwegian influence.

By the mid-eighteenth century, foreign influences affected the simple, refreshing patterns. From Holland, for instance, came its ubiquitous tulip (the earliest tulip found in Finland was painted on the door of a small safe and dates back to 1685). But the tulip was hardly a common motif and it seems never to have appeared on textiles until the mid-eighteenth century. When the tulip form did appear as a rug design, it was diffused with other motifs, taking a less significant role within the pattern. By 1786, a number of rugs were decorated with the tulip and a palmetto, another foreign motif, this time from the Middle East brought to Finland by way of Germany. Keys, as a symbol, superseded the tulip in borders.

By 1804, windmills, horns, and vases of flowers appeared. Many of these patterns were brought to Finland by soldiers who brought gifts to their families after long campaigns overseas. Often the motif was found painted or woven in textiles.

It was not until the late eighteenth century that European Baroque or Rococo patterns found their way north. Finland, still under the domination of Sweden, was ruled by the Francophile Gustavus III (1771–1792) who brought to the Swedish court artists and designers from France. These men exposed the northern peoples to other symbols and devices, such as the heraldic lion (now a part of the Finnish coat of arms), the laurel wreath, flower pots and vases (originally by way of Italy to France)—all part of the Rococo inheritance, which ceased as quickly as it started about 1840. Other designs, such as the elk, probably came from Norway by way of the Hanseatic League (a German shipping union plying the Northern Baltic seas). There were also "carnation" rugs, found earlier in both Sweden and Germany.

Immediately following this period was the Romantic Period, when the handicrafts in general began to decline, losing all their originality and charm. The fresh spirit of the early folk designs and natural patterns gave way to impressionism and diffusion. For the collector today, rya rugs dating from this mid-nineteenth century period of romanticism, have little or no value.

Scandinavia, 1784, rya. Area of Karkku. *Photo: Weeks.*

Scandinavia, 1785, rya. Area of Juupa-joki. *Photo: Weeks. Galerie Hörham-mer, Helsinki.*

Scandinavia, 1799, rya. Area of Myr-skylä. *Photo: Weeks. Suomi Kansallis Museo.*

142

Scandinavia, 1799, rya. Area of Erärvi. *Galerie Hörhammer, Helsinki.*

Scandinavia, 18th century (?), rya. Area of Akää. *Photo: Weeks. Galerie Hörhammer, Helsinki.*

Scandinavia, late 18th century (?), rya. Area of Säärijärvi. *Photo: Weeks. Galerie Hörhammer, Helsinki.*

144

Scandinavia, 18th century, rya. Area of Hauho. *Photo: Weeks. Galerie Hör-hammer, Helsinki.*

Scandinavia, 1802, rya. Area of Kuorevesi. *Photo: Weeks.*

Scandinavia, 1805, rya. Area of Karjolohja. *Photo: Weeks. Private Collection, Helsinki.*

Scandinavia, 1805, rya. Area of Kylmäkosken. *Galerie Hörhammer, Helsinki.*

Scandinavia, 1811, rya. Area of Ylöjärvi. *Photo: Weeks. Galerie Hörhammer, Helsinki.*

148

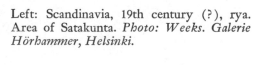

Left: Scandinavia, 19th century (?), rya. Area of Satakunta. *Photo: Weeks. Galerie Hörhammer, Helsinki.*

Right: Scandinavia, 19th century (?), rya. Area of Siikainen. *Photo: Weeks.*

Left: Scandinavia, 1826, rya. Area of Längelmäen. *Collection Leon Polak, Berlin.*

Scandinavia, early 19th century (?), rya. Area of Kuhmoisten.

5 GREECE

Greek Islands. Needlepoint carpet with the design taken from an old embroidery. Carnation pattern, traditional pattern of Epirus. *Photo: Weeks. Courtesy of the Greek Island Ltd. Collection.*

THE CRAFTS of the small islands off the coast of Greece are perhaps more typically Greek in character than those of the mainland. In the past, Greece proper has been invaded from the north so frequently that its crafts, including woven textiles and embroideries, reflect a Balkan tradition, whereas those found on the islands still have distinct traditions of their own. This is in spite of the fact that most of the islands have from time to time been inhabited by people other than Greek. But on each island the craftsmen have managed to refashion the many mixed design origins and make them into something quite unique in expression, and generally speaking, the peasant arts of the Greek Islands, if they have not remained the same, have maintained a great similarity with those of several generations past. Patterns and the many types of weaves and emboideries have consistently been passed down from mother to daughter, with only minor adaptations by each of the individual weavers. With the possible exception of Crete, very few rugs or embroideries have been dated.

There is an old Greek tradition and superstition attached to the use of thread and to the act of weaving, and according to popular belief a piece of red thread can avert any natural or supernatural menace, illness, or the evil

153

eye. The Director of the Museum of Greek Popular Art, Popi Zora, tells us that when a girl is born into a peasant family, a distaff is placed under her pillow so that she will grow up to be a hard worker. In some parts of Greece, to dispell illness, they throw a spindle high in the air, uttering incantations while doing so, or else they hang spindles on the branches of a willow tree. Elsewhere it is one of the customs surrounding a wedding that when the bride enters her new home she is offered a spindle and distaff with a full load of wool.

Since Greece traditionally has been a wool producing country, women developed their weaving skills many centuries ago. Originally the woven and embroidered rugs of the country were essentially for use as bedcovers, at times as hangings, but more often for the daughter's dower chests. The patterns of these rugs varied considerably from island to island, and apart from an occasional intermarriage, there seems to have been little intermingling of each island's style or design. It therefore becomes reasonably simple for the student to identify patterns from each of the many islands. Not all islands produced rugs, but all did produce beautiful embroideries for tables, windows, pillows, etc., as well as for clothing. The variations of these embroideries, and of the woven or embroidered rugs, are both technically and esthetically limitless, with the artistic styles of each region being only slightly colored by the island's own history.

Over the years, many outside influences have come from Byzantium, Persia, Turkey, and Western Europe. But by far the most influential were those from Byzantium, itself a mixture of east and west. The Eastern influence was largely from Syria and Sassanian Persia, the latter so evident in Byzantine textiles. The geometric designs of the Cyclades Islands, for instance, most certainly have come from the East. Many animal forms having their origins in Mesopotamia and the tree of life or *hom* motif, when it appears supported by animals or birds, came to the islands from Byzantium and Sassanian Persia. Another Persian design which occurs with some frequency is the carnation. It is, however, interesting to note that none of the rug patterns have anything in common with modern Persian designs.

In modern times, as is natural, Turkish influences have been felt more strongly on those islands nearest the Turkish coast. Epirus came under Turkish rule with the rest of the Greek mainland in the fifteenth century, at which time it had a Moslem population. Herringbone patterns found on Jannina have a distinct Turkish flavor. Other islands incorporated Turkish forms, re-designing them into something new, having a more Greek flavor. Flower patterns came to Greece by way of Turkey, which owed its floral patterns mainly to the textile weavers of Safavid Persia.

Western influence in the Aegean was established by the Crusaders, made up of French, Catalan, and Italians who sacked Byzantium in 1204 and partitioned the Byzantine Empire before moving on to Greece during the thirteenth to the fifteenth centuries. Certain animal motifs used in all the island designs are heraldic in character and may have been taken from the Crusaders who in turn were undoubtedly influenced by Middle Eastern styles. It is hard to tell.

During the occupation of the Crusaders, the Knights of St. John were established on Rhodes, while other islands came under the rule of the Venetians or Genoese from Italy and remained so until the Turkish conquest. The Ionian Islands remained under Venetian domination for a much longer time, in fact, as late as 1797, when Napoleon broke up the Venetian Republic. From 1815 to 1864 these same islands came under the British Protectorate before being turned back to Greece. Unlike the Aegean islands, these Ionian islands never came under Turkish rule. But in spite of the length of these various western occupations, textile patterns have never reflected a western influence with the possible exception of Crete.

As traditionalism and patriotism are essential to any peasant art, it is possible that the static life of these women on the Greek Islands led to a refinement of early folk lore and to an identification with the old craft forms and patterns. This might explain why so few generations of weavers or embroiderers were affected by these many outside pressures. Instead they selected only a few symbols or motifs for their designs. Although the English women reached out to nature and to their own flower gardens for inspiration, Greek women steadfastly clung to their own heritage of designs passed down from mother to daughter and dating from unknown times. Sometimes these patterns came by way of other types of textiles, or from designs painted on pottery. In certain villages patterns had homely names, such as "walnut" or "hen," not because these motifs were used *per se*, but because some abstract form reminded the weaver of these familiar objects.

Early rugs were muted in color because of the vegetable dyes available. The rather strong and sometimes garish colors which have appeared in some modern rugs are due to the easier-to-use aniline dyes readily purchasable in the market. Some islands became famous for their own dyes, such as the red from the island of Amorgos, or the green of Karpathos. But in general, the vegetable dyes insured that there were no strident tones. The weaver's eye for the restrained blending of colors within one rug allowed him to introduce at times brilliant flashes of color without upsetting the scheme. Often bright cyclamen pink would appear within a design predominantly brick red, for instance, and as strident as it may seem, these insertions never irritated the viewer. On the whole, colors had a clarity of their own. The exception was on the island of Crete, where at times colors were unashamedly flamboyant. But of the many colors available, red was by far the most popular on all of the islands. Yellow, usually soft in tone, was also used everywhere, but a bright lemon yellow is typical of Creton weaves and embroideries. Blue belongs to the Cyclades and Dodecanese, a paler blue in the northern Sporades; but darker or navy blue comes from Crete. Natural wool colors—white, gray, or a brownish black—were often used as ground colors of the rugs. Where a deep, clear black appears the wool has been dyed.

Quite a number of human figures have made their way into the woven and embroidered rugs. In Crete a small soldier, the "Evzone" figure with his full white skirt and red pompoms is not uncommon. Animals and birds are scattered about on a number of rugs. In particular is the peacock, which, although often stylized, is not difficult to recognize. The peacock has for centuries been used as an ornamental design all over the Middle East because of the legend about the incorruptibility of its flesh. It is also considered a symbol of longevity. The Byzantine church considered the peacock as the symbol of immortality, and we have been told that St. Augustine once took home from a dinner party a small piece of peacock meat to test the truth of the tale. The peacock has been found supporting the tree of life on a few embroideries found on some islands. In the work of many of the island weavers or embroiderers, the tree of life may be so abstracted that it is hard to interpret, but the peacock is always naturalistic enough to be recognizable. On Crete the peacock is generally naturalistic in appearance. Another bird, the double-headed Byzantine eagle, has been associated in the minds of Cretans with the former glory of Greece, and the stag, once the symbol of Rhodes, can also be found in Ionian island designs.

Many geometric forms appear throughout the islands and include the *glastra* (flower pot), which rarely appears as a vase for flowers, but rather as an interesting geometric form. This somehow seems to have been connected with the tree of life symbolism. The *wace* refers to the hexagon and diamond border.

The Kilim

Of the many types of weaves found in rugs and carpets, the tapestry weave is one of the most universal, appearing over many centuries in countries of the most diverse cultural backgrounds. In the Near East, rugs and carpets woven with this flat-weave tapestry stitch are *"Kilims."* This is a type of rug or carpet which predates those pile carpets which have been knotted with the so-called ghiordes knot. Few Kilims have been woven for commercial use; rather they have been woven by native craftsmen, often members of nomadic tribes ranging the countryside of Persia, Turkey, and Greece. Actually, Kilims have been found in as far and diverse or unlikely places as Sarajevo in Bosnia and in Western Bulgaria. The many Kilims woven, however, were not necessarily for use as rugs, but instead as door hangings at the entrance of tents or small huts, as wrappings for family treasures, or as covers to sleep under. Those Kilims woven throughout the Balkans tended to mimic designs and colors of Orientals from Asia. Those found in Greece, and particularly in the islands, more often remained the color of the natural wool or were red and decorated with repeat patterns or with embroidery in bright wools. The embroidery was applied simultaneously with the weaving process, not applied later as one might think. Almost all of the Greek Kilims were of wool, but occasionally goat's hair was added to make the rug waterproof.

The Flokati

The Greek word *floko* means "strand" and the Flokati has a very long pile of sheep's wool. These fluffy rugs have no pattern, depending instead on the dense thickness of the pile and bright color as their only decorative element. Today's Flokatis are woven and dyed in the same manner as they have been for generations. The yarn is twisted on special hand spindles, which gives it the loose fluffy texture. The yarn is then woven on hand looms into a mat-like base, leaving the strands loose to create a pile—sometimes as long as six inches. After weaving, the rugs are removed from the looms and taken to local natural waterfalls for several hours. The crystal waters cascading down in billowing torrents purify and soften the wool fibers, leaving the rug wonderfully soft. The rug is then dyed.

The Cretan Kouskousse

Rugs of this type are embroidered. Perhaps the most significant characteristic is the raised popcorn-like balls of embroidery generally found, making a symmetrical pattern to this otherwise flat surface. The Kouskousse is most generally found in the off-white natural color of the sheep's wool; a few modern Kouskousses have been dyed, and occasionally black and white ones have been found.

COLOR ILLUSTRATIONS

Spanish rug of the late 17th century. *The Hispanic Society of America.*

Woolen pile rug, Spanish, of the 16th century. *The Hispanic Society of America.*

17th century woolen pile rug of Cuenca. *The Hispanic Society of America.*

Cuenca rug of the late 17th century or early 18th century. *The Hispanic Society of America.*

Spain

Spanish rug of the 17th century. *The Hispanic Society of America.*

16th century Spanish Wreath rug. *The Hispanic Society of America.*

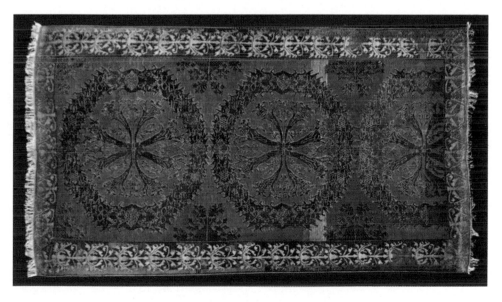

France

The bedroom of Louis XIV
in the Grand Trianon,
Versailles.

The dining room of the
Grand Trianon.

Napoleon's Green Salon in the Grand Trianon.

Great Britain

Great Britain: Power-machine-woven carpet, circa 1850. Woven for the Exposition of 1850-51 at the Crystal Palace, Hyde Park, London, by Crossley Carpets.

Scandinavia

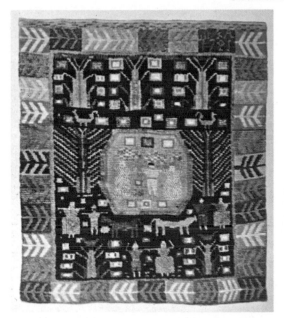

Scandinavian carpet, circa 1721, Saarijärei. *Photo by Jeanne G. Weeks.*

Scandinavian carpet of 1711. *Photo by Jeanne G. Weeks.*

1790 Soärjarvi carpet. *Photo by Jeanne G. Weeks.*

Scandinavia

Koyliö carpet, circa 1807.
Photo by Jeanne G. Weeks.

Carpet, circa 1806, Hameenkyrö.
Photo by Jeanne G. Weeks.

Pälkäne carpet, date unknown. *Photo by Jeanne G. Weeks.*

Greek Islands

Left: Evzone (soldier figure) rug, flat weave. Note the cross design and the initials of the weaver (KOK) which have been woven backwards. Hook design shows Turkish influence, but colors of rug are brilliant, not subtle as Turkish colorations. About thirty years old. *Collection of Marian Miller. Photo by Jeanne G. Weeks.*

Above: Crete, Greek Islands. Flat weave rug with cross, star and flowers—all typical designs. Butterfly in center is more unusual. About sixty years old. *Collection of Marian Miller. Photo by Jeanne G. Weeks.*

Left: Greek island rug, Crete. "Church" design embroidered on the loom. Typical design about thirty years old. *Collection of Marian Miller. Photo by Jeanne G. Weeks.*

American

Left: American hook rug, circa 1850.
Courtesy Museum of American
Folk Art. Photo by Jeanne G. Weeks.

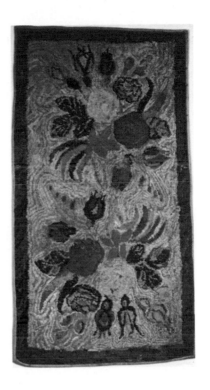

Above: Early 19th
century American hook
rug. Courtesy of Museum
of American Folk Art,
Collection of Herbert W.
Hemphill, Jr. Photo by
Jeanne G. Weeks.

Late Victorian rug, circa 1880. Courtesy of Museum of
American Folk Art, Collection of Herbert W. Hemphill,
Jr. Photo by Jeanne G. Weeks.

Above: Very early 18th century American rug. Most unusual, probably a table mat, since it measures only eight by twelve inches. *Courtesy Museum of American Folk Art, Collection of Herbert W. Hemphill, Jr. Photo by Jeanne G. Weeks.*

Right: New England "Turkey" rug hooked to imitate an Oriental Ghiorde pattern. Probably 19th century. *Old Sturbridge Village Photo. Collection of Nina Fletcher Little.*

New England shirred rug, vine pattern, composed of tightly rolled felt strips. Probably 18th century. *Old Sturbridge Village Photo. Collection of Nina Fletcher Little.*

Navajo rug from Two Gray Hills Post. Contemporary. *Contemporary Navajo rugs from the American Indian Arts Center, New York. Photo by Jeanne G. Weeks.*

American Indian

Rug made in Bluff, Arizona, in the style of Two Gray Hills. *Contemporary Navajo rugs from the American Indian Arts Center, New York. Photo by Jeanne G. Weeks.*

Yei rug from the Shiprock area; yarns vegetal-dyed. *Contemporary Navajo rugs from the American Indian Arts Center, New York. Photo by Jeanne G. Weeks.*

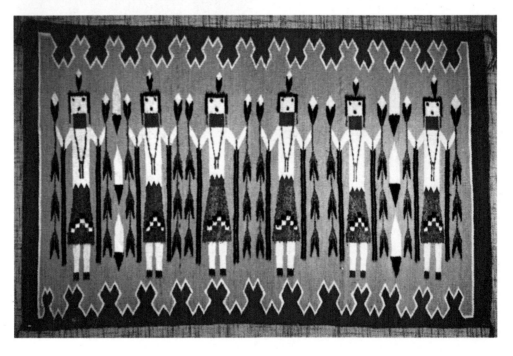

American Indian

Crystal rug in an earlier style; yarns dyed with aniline dyes. *Contemporary Navajo rugs from the American Indian Arts Center, New York. Photo by Jeanne G. Weeks.*

Sandpainting rug. Four water-animal figures, horned toads, and a messenger fly partially surrounded by a rainbow figure; other figures represent corn, beans, squash, tobacco. This painting represents the Beauty Way Chant—a ceremony to purify the body or spirit from non-Indian or non-Navajo influences. *Contemporary Navajo rugs from the American Indian Arts Center, New York. Photo by Jeanne G. Weeks.*

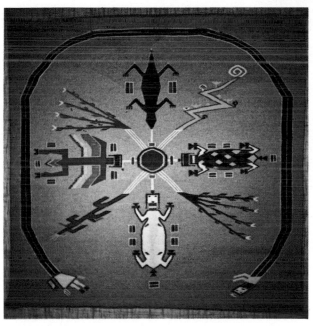

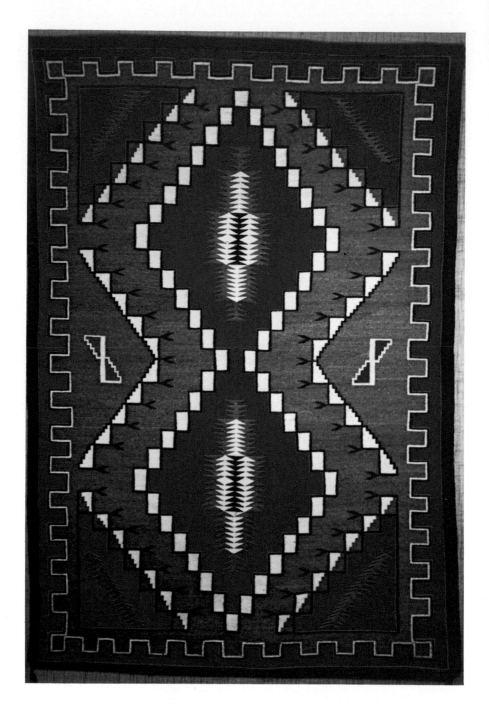

Ganado Red. *Contemporary Navajo rugs from the American Indian Arts Center, New York. Photo by Jeanne G. Weeks.*

Left: Greek Islands. Needlepoint. Traditional Greek design, showing "Skyros Boats." *Photo: Weeks. Courtesy of Greek Island Ltd. Collection.*

Above: Greek Islands. Flat weave carpet, the Kilim from Northern Greece and Macedonia. *Photo: Weeks. Courtesy of Greek Island Ltd. Collection.*

Left: Greek Islands. Crete. Embroidered on the loom over flat weave. Traditional "Church" pattern. *Photo: Weeks. Courtesy of Greek Island Ltd. Collection.*

Opposite page: Greek Islands. Crete, area of Sfakiana. Embroidered on the loom over flat weave. *Photo: Weeks. Courtesy of Greek Island Ltd. Collection.*

Greek Islands. Kilim from the village of Olympos, Thessaly.

Top, left: Greek Islands. Crete. Embroidered on the loom over a flat weave. "Church Pattern," traditional. *Photo: Weeks.*

Top, right: Greek Islands. Kilim from the village of Pilion, Thessaly.

Above: Greek Islands. Crete. Border detail. Embroidered on the loom. *Photo: Weeks.*

Left: Greek Islands. Crete. Traditional pattern embroidered on the loom. *Photo: Weeks. Courtesy of Greek Island Ltd. Collection.*

Greek Islands. Kilim from the village of Pilion, Thessaly.

Greek Islands. Kilim from the area of Almyros, Thessaly.

Greek Islands. Crete. Detail of embroidered carpet embroidered on loom over flat weave. *Courtesy of Harmony Carpets.*

Greek Islands. Crete. Small rug embroidered on loom over flat weave.

Greek Islands. Kouskousse of natural off-white.
Collection of Harmony Carpets.

Greek Islands. Kouskousse of natural off-white
(detail). *Collection of Harmony Carpets.*

Crete. Embroidered on the loom, red. *Collection of Harmony Carpets.*

Crete. Embroidered on the loom, red. *Collection of Harmony Carpets.*

Crete. Embroidered on the loom, small. *Collection of Harmony Carpets.*

Greek Islands. Kouskousse of natural black and white. *Collection of Harmony Carpets.*

Below, left: Greek Islands. Flokati of off-white. *Collection of Harmony Carpets.*

Below, right: Greek Islands. Flokati of off-white (detail). *Collection of Harmony Carpets.*

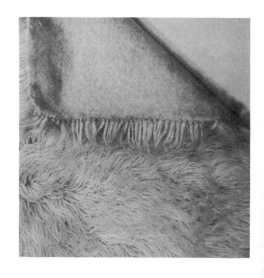

6 AMERICA

American, New England. Yarn
sewn rug of unusual geometric
pattern. Home dyed woolen
yarn on linen. 18th century (?)
Old Sturbridge Village photo.
*Collection of Nina Fletcher
Little.*

T HE EARLY CRAFTS of America owe much to the many
cultural heritages brought by immigrants from a number of fatherlands. But
the majority of those who established settlements in New England and Virginia, the most progressive of the early colonies, came from England.

By the late seventeenth and early eighteenth centuries, many other small,
isolated, but nonetheless vigorous, settlements grew up along the Eastern coast
of the country and were made up of Dutch, French, Spanish, German, and
Swedish each group adhering with great tenacity to its own cultural heritage. Then during the nineteenth century, a number of other groups, the
Irish, Italian, Russian, and Balkan, arrived. Only great strength and courage
enabled them to survive the tedious voyage to this country in the badly
ventilated holds of those small sailing vessels. It has been said, in fact, that
America was made up of "persons of quality, emigrants, religious exiles,
political rebels, serving men sold for a term of years, apprentices, children
stolen, maidens pressed and others." But regardless of their need or background, all were searching for a better way of life, an opportunity to build
a home and establish themselves within an orderly community.

In spite of the diversity of backgrounds, more than fifty per cent of   173 today's population still stems from English traditions, and it is this cultural heritage which has predominated in almost all early American crafts.

By 1666, the glacial rocks of New England had been cleared from the land and small, rural farms had been cultivated. The Indians had been fought and contained. In towns, independent churches, the hub of thought and influence, had been established. Trade had developed with Europe, and in general those rugged and hard-working people were able to settle down to enjoy a sociable existence.

To the south, large plantations had been given by King's grant to wealthy sons of English noble families, and sweeping, fertile pasture lands were bearing fruits of the harvest: cotton, tobacco, rice, indigo, and feed for the horses—many products for export. The fields were harvested by slaves brought to the country for that purpose. Unlike the colonists of New England, Virginians brought with them traditions of easy living and the pursuits of the country gentlemen. One of their main activities was the raising of fine horses for the hunt and for exhibition. The Virginians built beautiful houses and graced them with handsome furnishings, all imported, for these people occupied themselves with the charms of hospitality built around a social and political life. A beautiful home was a necessity for those seeking status.

The period between 1666 and the early eighteenth century was one of consolidation for the country. There was relative peace in Europe and fewer immigrants left their country for the new land and opportunity. In New England the rhythm of the farmer's life was interrupted only by rugged and destructive winters, a time when life was spent indoors around the warm fireplace. But the farmers were poor and had little money to spend on furnishings for their homes or even to make them comfortable. What furnishings they had were often made by their own hand or by local craftsmen. The most primitive houses had earthen floors, hardened by the many feet walking over them. But these were cold and damp, so for insulation rushes, herbs, or sweet fragrant ferns were scattered over the floor. For those homes which had wide, pine wood plank floors, floorcoverings of plaited, woven, or loose straw were used. Listed in several inventories was an herb or plant called "feathergrass," and another, "Spanish rush." Both were used to make mats. In other homes sand was used, sifted each morning through a sand sieve, sometimes smoothed with a hair or hemlock broom into quaint circles, herringbone patterns, or fancy wreaths—an agreeable task for the artistic chambermaid. Unfortunately, these charming patterns lasted only a short time, for once walked on, they immediately became disarrayed. By the end of the day a home with a large family must have looked quite messy. But it seems that sand was plentiful and readily available in some cities from the street corner vendor.

At a very early date American women began making hooked or braided rugs for their homes. (Samples of their work still existing date back to the early eighteenth century.) Although these small rugs were made throughout the thirteen colonies, New England led in the craft of hooking rugs, which most certainly had the priority over braided rugs. Perhaps it was the long winters with much snow that kept the housewife working by the warm fireside—or perhaps it was a natural Scottish-English thriftiness which made her save enough small cuttings of material that had to be utilized somehow.

Further south, where the climate was warmer, those people who had wealth imported many of their rugs. Virginians, in particular, raised cotton and tobacco for export to England, and credit was established there against which the family could purchase household luxuries through agents or friends—not always with success. One letter of indignation dated August 7, 1773 was written by a Thomas Nelson, Jr., of Virginia:

Gentlemen, Captain Robertson delivered your letter for the floor cloth and anchovies. The cloth is injur'd by being rolled before the paint was dry, and the anchovies were very fine for which Mrs. Nelson returns you her particular thanks.

(The paint refers to a type of painted canvas carpet popular as a floorcovering in the eighteenth century, a type of carpet which we will mention in more detail later in this chapter.)

One cannot help but have great admiration for the courageous farmer's wives of New England, who with limited resources toiled long nights to make something beautiful for their frugal homes. The designs, limited only by their own imagination, were colorful and showed considerable creative vitality.

The material came from left-over scraps of fabric or from old clothing—material woven at home from flax sowed in the spring and harvested in the fall, or from wool clipped from sheep in the meadow. The wool was carded, spun, and woven by members of the family. The sound of the hand loom was a familiar one in many farmhouses. The cloths produced by such tedious labor were highly prized and were often passed down to daughters for their own homes. In 1767 Sir Henry Moore, Governor of New York, commented to the British Board of Trade on

. . . the custom of making coarse cloth in private families without the slightest sign of sending it to any market . . . every house swarms with children who are set to work as soon as they can spin or card, and as every family are furnished with a loom, the itinerant weavers who travel about the country put the finishing touch to the work.

It was the hooking or braiding of rugs which gave the housewife solace and a deep sense of fulfillment as she sat up late by the fireside after the strenuous chores of the day were completed. Actually there were a wide variety of types of rugs which could be made other than those popular hooked or braided ones. There were tongue-work door mats, dollar rugs, rag rugs (woven), patchwork rugs, and crocheted rugs. The most pictorial and colorful were, of course, the hooked and embroidered rugs. Hooked rugs were made on a frame with a thickly woven homespun or coarse linen (much later, burlap) material stretched tightly over it. Patterns were drawn on the fabric with a charcoal stick from the fire, or a piece of indigo. (These were sometimes referred to as "drawn-work" rugs.) In early hooked rugs the design was hooked in with strips of wool cloth (cotton was not imported from England until 1760). Hand-woven suiting was not suitable because it could not be cut into the small strips needed to pull through the ground fabric. Canadians sometimes mixed suiting with woolen yarns, for an interesting though rough texture in the finished piece. In general, however, the lighter fabrics or yarns, easily dyed, made the most evenly textured and attractive rugs. These various color fabric strips were cut into ⅜- or ½-inch widths and pulled through the cloth with a hook. The loops were raised slightly (approximately a half inch) on the surface side but seldom cut. The back, or underside, was kept flat. The closer the pile loops, the sturdier the rug. Home-dyed fabrics retained their brilliance to an amazing degree. Especially lasting were the reds, blues, and greens. Yellow-green faded easily, and home-dyed blacks have since turned rusty or greenish, whereas browns have retained a lustrous color; white mellowed to a soft ivory.

There were many charming domestic patterns. Borders had shell and scallop patterns, both easy to draw—an embellishment on the simple arc form. Others were "marbleized," or had waves. Central motifs included the diamond or star patterns, lozenge forms, overlapping circles, mosaic patterns, pictorial designs, and many variations on leaf forms. Flowers appeared in unending array, sometimes in bouquets, singly, or in combinations. During the Victorian era, large, full-petalled roses bloomed with brilliant and deep colors.

Lilies, forget-me-nots, bleeding hearts—all the beloved flowers of the summer garden—were recreated with nostalgia during the long, cold winter nights.

Picture rugs illustrated barnyards and snow scenes, affording more personal glimpses of the home life. Cats were particularly popular and were drawn sleeping near the hearth or playing with their kittens. Trusty dogs guarded the home, or the farmer's faithful horse was shown waiting under the apple tree or at the gate. Horse-shoe patterns were for good luck, and on occasion there was the biblical lion.

Wives living in sea coast towns, who patiently waited for the return of a husband, would hook pictures of the sea, full-rigged ships, whaling parties, or anchors.

Dates rarely appeared on hooked rugs, but many an initial and sometimes full names were carefully hooked into corners or along one end. A few motto rugs have appeared somewhat resembling those homey samplers bearing sentiments of "Home Sweet Home," "Welcome," or "Call Again."

Pre-stamped patterns could be found in embroidery books made in Germantown, Pennsylvania, but the accompanying wool came in poor or harsh color schemes. Classrooms turned out theorems to be hooked by groups of school girls. Early patterns were repeated by later generations within the same family, leaving us with an assortment of duplicates as well as originals.

One enterprising pedlar, E. S. Frost of Biddeford, Maine, was able to capitalize on the prevailing interest during the years 1868–1876 by creating patterned zinc stencils with which he stamped canvases with a number of designs—flowers, scrolls, or animal forms. These are easily recognizable to-day, for also stamped in the corner are the words "E. Frost & Company, Biddeford, Maine."

A simpler rug to make with old or discarded bits of material was the knitted rug. Here narrow strips of fabric were cut and sewn together lengthwise, then wound into small balls like string ready to be knitted. This process antedated the crocheting of rugs, which used the same type of fabric ball. These were hooked with a crochet needle. A variation of the crochet rug was the "fluff" mat. This was made by cutting the fabrics into small strips about ½ to 2½ inches long (depending on the thickness of the fabric) and crocheting them into a burlap or foundation cloth. Heavy crochet thread caught the fabric strips in the middle and secured them to the burlap, leaving the ends free. This gave a short overall pile to the mat.

The more primitive tongue rug was usually of door-mat size and was made up of snippets of cloth three inches wide by about five inches long and rounded at one end. These pieces were blanket-stitched with colorful wool yarns around the edges (to keep them from raveling). The straight narrow end of each piece was then sewn onto a sturdy foundation cloth or burlap. The small pieces were overlapped in straight rows, beginning at the outer edge and working to the center. The fabric was often the remains of a husband's or son's worn-out suit.

Similar to the tongue rug were button or dollar rugs in which small, rounded pieces of fabric, about the size of a silver dollar, were sewn to a foundation cloth. These were arranged in rows just touching each other. Sometimes the pattern was varied by alternating several sizes of discs and different colors.

More beautiful and more inventive were the patchwork rugs made by applying small pieces of lively colored cloth cut out in the shapes of flowers, leaves, vines, or other motifs and applied to a heavy, black or dark colored cloth. These ornamental patterns were used individually, in clusters, or as repeat patterns, and they showed up to considerable advantage against the dark ground cloth.

Rag rugs were woven on hand looms. Pieces of cotton, linen, or woolen cloth were cut into strips and were woven into fine linen thread warps. Often bright materials were used, and a few inches of the warp was left dangling at either end to be knotted into fringes. These were particularly popular during the Early American period.

Braided rugs were also found in abundance at about the same time. These were made of three strands of narrow bands of cloth, ¼ to 1¼ inches wide. As these were plaited together, the raw edges of the strips were turned in. This required some skill as the tension had to remain the same throughout the process to prevent the whole rug from puckering when sewn together. Finished braids were sewn together in circles or ovals, although a few examples of square, rectangular, or cloverleaf rugs do exist. (These latter shapes generally had a center portion of parallel rows mitered at the corners.) For wider, thicker rugs, up to eight by twelve inches, strands of fabric could be plaited together. Rugs of men's torn suiting, though durable, were generally dark or sombre in color. Those from New Hampshire usually were shaded with light colors in the center, ranging to darker ones at the edges.

By far the most elaborate and imaginative were the embroidered or cross-stitched rugs which seemed rare in early days but appeared with great frequency during the latter part of the eighteenth and early nineteenth centuries. Work in tent and cross-stitch undoubtedly had been done from early times, but the most exotic floral imitation Orientals ("Turkey work") made in seventeenth century England were apparently not copied in America until later. The American ones were made of wool embroidery threads sewn into a coarse canvas foundation. The best known, large-scale embroidered rug was made by Zurich Higley Guernsey of Castletown, Vermont. She took at least two years to make her parlor rug, for she first sheared the wool from the sheep in her father's flock. It was finished in 1835. The rug— certainly more of a carpet than rug size—was twelve by thirteen and a half feet and consisted of a number of individually designed squares embroidered on a coarse homespun ground cloth with a chain stitch. Later the squares were sewn together. The patterns were basically in the eighteenth-century tradition, but a few, like that of a cat, seem to have been a Victorian precursor of the style.

Shaker rugs were made up of bits of homespun rags strung like beads onto threads, then sewn to a heavy round or square canvas until the surface was completely covered. Pure line and form of naturalistic designs were alien to the intensely religious spirit of these people who had rejected most art forms. Designs, therefore, remained abstract or symbolic, yet in good taste sympathetic to the simple attitudes of the community. When animals did appear in their rug designs, and that was infrequently, little differentiation was made between a dog or cow. More usual were borders of contrasting colored stripes, waves, or other simple geometric forms.

Some cross-stitch and other types of rugs, embellished with traditional needlework designs, were made in some segments of the country. Both the Pennsylvania Dutch and German settlers brought with them a tradition of fine embroidery, and some of the more beautiful examples of rugs come from these groups. A few pieces of embroidery also survive from the Dutch pioneers of New York along the Hudson River. But not all of these works were used as rugs. Many were used as table-top covers, wall hangings, and window coverings. One cross-stitch carpet, now in the possession of the Metropolitan Museum, measuring 18'8" by 15'8", was made on the estate of Judge Pliny Moore (1808–1812) in Champlain, New York. It was a gift to the Museum by a Mrs. Isabelle Mygatt, who sent with it the following story.

The plan of making a carpet projected by my grandmother, Martha Corbin Moore, wife of Judge Pliny Moore, of Champlain, who was a man of means, and who sent her daughters to Montreal to a catholic Convent to study French and be instructed in needlework embroidery—learned 28 different stitches. At the time no woven carpets were brought as far north as Canada, so grandmother conceived of the idea of embroidering a carpet for the drawing room about 28-feet square. Although every article used was raised on the estate, from wool on the sheep through the process of manufacturing the thread, to coloring of the soft yarns for embroidery. There was no canvas obtainable at home. Material was sent from Montreal. Frame made of planed boards, canvas 18 inches across set diagonally, divided by 6-inch bands of bronze roses. After main breadths of carpet were done, workers perplexed by border, adapted design from cotton handkerchief, stamped with border of shells, which were the stock of a peddler. Four years occupied in the making; begun in 1808, completed in 1812. Lining woven on loom in grandmother's kitchen, made of flax, grown on the estate. Fireplace rug 6'2" made for the carpet, had similar borders, but narrower center design being two hounds in pursuit of deer. The rug was given by Mrs. Hubbell (daughter of Mrs. Moore) to her second daughter, Mrs. Seymour. (signed) Martha A. Mygatt, Chazy, June 19, 1908.

If there were fancier needlework rugs made in America during the eighteenth century, we have little or no evidence of it today. For stylistically, all rugs made at home were basically primitive. They did, however, have one virtue in common—all cost little or nothing to make. But of all the rugs made, the hooked rug seems to have been most compatible and contemporary to eighteenth-century furniture.

Prior to the Revolution, America could boast of more than three million people within her colonies, and within the growing cities located along the Eastern coast, an affluent middle class was developing. No domestic woven carpets of quality showed up prior to the mid-eighteenth century; in fact, the use of carpets was exceptional, and those that did appear in the homes of the wealthy in Virginia, Philadelphia, or Boston were imported from England or France. These carpets as well as other household luxuries were treated with great esteem.

There were no factories prior to the eighteenth century, and for those who were not able, or did not choose, to import their carpets, there were several alternate solutions, the most attractive of which were floor cloths of canvas, sail cloth, or some other sturdy cloth covered with several coats of paint for durability. These were imported from England or made domestically. (It was in reference to one of these types of floor cloth that Thomas Nelson Jr. of Virginia was piqued to the point of writing his letter of complaint dated August of 1773. See page 175.)

Domestic floor cloths were generally made by a local professional who, as a house painter, plied his craft equally among the painting of floor cloths, signs and houses, and who more often than not also sold paints and related supplies. According to one newspaper advertisement, upholsterers and paperhangers also manufactured floor cloths, or repaired worn or faded ones. When patterns wore thin, they were simply repainted.

The designs were varied ranging from plain and solid colors to marbleized effects. Popular were dominoes, octagons, squares, or cubed patterns—nearly all in repeat formation—painted in several colors to allow for dimensional effects. Some had borders. Others had allover figured designs.

These painted canvases, or floor cloths, were not exclusive with the poor or middle class, although they probably offered the widest range of prices for varied budgets. Sturdier ones were used for entries and hallways; the lighter weight ones were used in the summertime, replacing the more valuable imported and fancy wool-pile or Orientals of wintertime. Use of these floor cloths continued until long after the Revolution.

It seems that even Thomas Jefferson in later years used a canvas floor cloth painted green in a small front dining room in the White House; and in the Great Hall entrance, the whole floor was covered with a canvas painted green. (This is according to Jefferson's inventory dated February 8, 1861, of "furniture in the President's House, the property of the United States.")

In homes where the housewife was creative, more imaginative designs could be worked out, and such a one was created by the bride of Lyman Beecher (as so delightfully recounted to his children in East Hampton).

We had no carpet; there was not a carpet from end to end of the town. All had sanded floors, some of them worn through. Your mother introduced the first carpet. Uncle Lot gave us some money, and I had an itch to spend it. Went to a vendue and bought a bale of cotton. She spun it, and had it woven; then she laid it down, sized it, and painted it in oils with a border all around and bunches of roses and other flowers over the center. She sent to New York for her colors and ground, and mixed them herself. The carpet was nailed down on the garrett floor, and she used to go up there to paint.

There was no hand-weaving industry in America such as those found in England, France, and Spain, until the mid-eighteenth century at which time a Philadelphian, Peter Sprague, set up looms to produce carpeting in the Axminster manner. The looms were narrow, and in order to make a large carpet, strips of this hand-woven carpeting had to be sewn together. The factory gave employment to poor women and to children who were trained to weave a fine quality of carpeting. Several of these carpets went to the White House, and in a report in the Philadelphia *Gazette of the United States*, dated June 22, 1701, it mentions that Sprague's "carpets made for the President and various other persons, are masterpieces of their kind, particularly that for the Senate Chamber of the United States." One was created for the Senate Chamber in Congress Hall, Philadelphia, with a

device woven in the *Crest* and *Armorial Achievements* appertaining to the *United States*. Thirteen stars forming a constellation diverging from a cloud, occupy the same space under the chair of the Vice-President. THE AMERICAN EAGLE is displayed in the center holding in his dexter talon an olive branch, in his sinister a bundle of thirteen arrows, and in his beak, a scroll inscribed with the motto, *E pluribus unum*. The whole being executed in a capital style, with rich bright colours, has a very fine effect.

Sprague was also reported to have made ingrain carpets as well as "Turkey"—undoubtedly similar to those made in England. His success was attributed to a certain growing sophistication and awareness on the part of urban Americans who wanted to be as fashionable as those in European countries.

Little mention is made of other hand-weaving establishments until 1884, when two Germans, both world travelers, endowed with an appreciation of the decorative arts, introduced looms they had brought with them from Germany. These they set up in Milwaukee, and for two years produced a limited number of small carpets in the German Renaissance style. At the end of that time, the looms were moved to a small factory in New York City specializing in very fine quality carpets of European style. The quality attracted a very chic and wealthy clientele. But despite this success, the New York company was fraught with many internal difficulties and finally, unable to compete with power-machine-made goods, closed its doors in 1905.

Early nineteenth century United States witnessed the same industrial expansion which had swept England. The initiator in this country was undoubtedly Eli Whitney, with his discovery of the cotton gin, followed closely by Fulton's harnessing of steam (in his case, of course, it was for that glamorous steamboat). These two acts following in close order had a tremendous impact, enough to revolutionize both social and economic life. America was growing up, developing a large middle or monied class eager for goods, particularly those which added to the amenities of life. Although home-made rugs were highly prized by many families, their use was hardly universal. To fulfill a growing demand for other types of carpeting, importers were bringing to this country rugs and carpets from Europe. By 1825 England was sending to east coast ports almost one-half million yards of carpeting. The American businessman could hardly stand aside and watch such a rich market be satisfied with imported goods. With an Emersonian ideal for self-reliance, the New England businessmen put their acumen and genius to the creation of a modern system of carpet manufacture. They invented and perfected a power loom which could transform a luxury product of the elite into a common necessity for all classes. The American carpet industry, which in a fairly short period of time became the most powerful in the world, in the beginning could only hope to fill its own domestic market.

Within a period of ten years (1825–1835), a dozen weaving mills were established, which included the Tariff Manufacturing Company, the Lowell Manufacturing Company, and Bigelow & Sanford. An unexpected boost to the newly formed industries was the tariff of 1824, which had set a 25¢ tax per square yard on finished carpeting from abroad while maintaining an earlier 15 per cent tax on imported raw wool. Four years later the "Tariff of Abomination," while only slightly increasing the tax on raw wool, nearly doubled that of the woven carpet.

The name of Lowell was outstanding, not only because it was the largest, but because it became famous for its "high standing, both socially and in its business point of view," and by introducing goods of "high character." But more important, Lowell made the first significant contribution and innovations to the American carpet industry, whereby they could reduce costs and increase capacity of production. The successful team behind the Lowell operation was a merchant, Frederick Cabot (a member of that illustrious Boston family), and a Scotch immigrant, Alexander Wright, a mechanic whose ancestors had been carpet weavers in Scotland. Wright went home to Scotland and with the aid of his relatives was able to gather up three hand looms and some twenty workers including a Peter Lawson, John Turnbull, and two Wright cousins, William and Claude Wilson.

Wright was successful in getting his equipment and men to this country in spite of a shipwreck en route. Soon he had established an operating mill on Chicken Brook in Medway, near Boston. The place, unfortunately, burned down a short while later, but the looms were salvageable and were moved to a small, single-story building nearby. An advertisement appeared in a local newspaper inviting prospective purchasers and others interested in machine processes to visit and see for themselves if the product was not "equal in every respect, if not superior, to the best [English] Kidderminster stuff." Ingrain was the product at the Lowell plant, as it was the least expensive and simplest to weave with little pattern. With this less expensive product, Lowell hoped to capture a large volume market. (Later, a few patterned Brussels and venetian carpets were produced there.) To turn out such a supply, larger additions were needed to house a dye house, drying shed, storeroom, and "countinghouse." In 1830 six Brussels hand looms, four venetian hand looms and one three-ply hand loom were added, and, as extra precaution, a fire engine was purchased.

On that early and momentous trip to Scotland, Wright had spent some time inquiring into power-driven looms. He was told only of forty years of failure. Not easily discouraged, Wright turned to Erastus Brigham Bigelow of Boston, the inventor of a mechanized coach-lace loom for the manufacture of a trimming on stagecoach upholstery. He tried to convince Bigelow of the benefits of inventing a power loom for the weaving of carpets. Bigelow turned his attentions to the considerable problems of the complex operation, one which could produce an ingrain material. But to succeed where others had failed he had many problems to resolve: how to set needles for the mechanical interweaving of two or three piles at a time, the provision of an accurate timing for the take-up beam of the fabric, how to create an even and firm selvedge, how to control the smooth surface with repeating patterns of uniform length so that they matched when seamed, and how to control the timing of a number of shuttle boxes.

Sufficient drawings were submitted to Wright within several weeks, and after some inspection the Lowell Manufacturing Company agreed to bear the expense for further experiment and for patenting, provided it was given the exclusive right to the machine. Royalty payments to Bigelow were set at two cents a yard until they reached $18 a week—a sum Bigelow was to consider his salary.

With Wright's help Bigelow started to improve his machine, which was too slow and was limited to producing only the simplest of patterns. Alterations delayed the delivery until December of 1843, at which time further changes delayed the use of the machine until late in 1846. These last changes lived up to expectations, with each loom producing up to twenty square yards a day of two-ply and fourteen square yards of three-ply goods. Bigelow's royalty was reduced to 1½¢ per square yard. But the success of the loom was to have a revolutionary effect on the industry. True, designs were restricted, but fortunately the esthetic tastes of a wide segment of the population had not developed sufficiently to notice. Patterns with large floriated scrolls were ideal for the serrations around the edges of the leaves and flowers, which "hid" the uneven joinings of the interchange of the colored threads. The Lowell patterns, under the direction of the firm's designer, Peter Lawson, were mainly composed of great blossoms with sweeping foliage asymmetrically arranged. (Some reporters denounced "the unnaturalness of walking on flowers" and recommended instead geometric patterns.)

The financial success of the Bigelow looms at the Lowell, Massachusetts, plant led other investors to establish other factories. In Connecticut two smaller mills, Tariff Manufacturing Company, the predecessor of the Bigelow-Sanford Company, and the Thompsonville Carpet Manufacturing Company were established. On December 5, 1826, the *Boston Daily Advertiser* reported,

We have just seen a piece of carpeting woven at Tariffville . . . by which appears that carpets can be made there of any colors and to any pattern, durable, cheap, and elegant. Coloring can be done as well in this country as in any other, and the weaving by the loom is of the right sort. The public will in a short time become acquainted with their carpets, and we only claim the credit of being the first to mention them. (An improvement apparently over those at Lowell.)

Another pioneer, John Sanford, of Mohawk Valley, a Congressman whose wealth was securely based in mercantile and real estate ventures, bought the Greene carpet factory. The factory had six looms (sent by sloop up the Hudson, then fifty miles on land by sleigh) and three experienced hand weavers. A few years later (in 1849) fire, a common hazard for all early New England mills, destroyed the plant. Undeterred, Sanford and his son built a new factory upstream, and by 1850, under the name John Sanford & Son, turned out not only ingrain carpets, but chenille carpets and rugs, plus rug yarns.

By 1846, the Lowell Company had not picked up their option for Bigelow's Brussels loom, content as they were with a successful ingrain business, the floorcovering of the middle class. Bigelow and his older brother, Horatio Nelson Bigelow, decided to set up their own factory to produce a pile carpet, a considerable refinement over the less expensive ingrain carpet. In April, 1850, the Bigelow Carpet Company opened with a total of fifty looms, modifications of the early Bigelow loom. By 1852, the Bigelow inventories listed a mill, dye house, reservoir, a well, plus the machinery and equipment. A few skilled workmen, all men, were supplemented with unskilled labor, mainly women, and by 1854, 195,000 yards of finished goods were produced annually.

During the hundred years or so which followed, the carpet industry grew, and due to the general vicissitudes of any industry, those companies which did not adopt new methods of manufacturing, merchandising, and not the least, fashion, faded from the scene. They were replaced by younger, more aggressive firms or were merged into the remaining old line firms. Toward the end of the century other weaves took precedence over the popular but stylistically limited ingrain carpet—the Axminster, the seamless carpet, the tapestry, velvet, and Wilton, all brought great gains for their innovators.

By 1914, a new market demanded much of the attention of the largest mills, the sale of contract goods for hotels, theatres, office buildings, and ships—wherever handsome appearance and long-wearing qualities were essential. These contracts were almost invariably obtained by cooperation with a dealer or jobber who would submit bids for large carpeting contracts. The mill's cooperation with its supplier might take the form of assisting in the design of special goods or of providing technical information on the types of floorcoverings suited for the project, and in enabling the bidder to quote an attractively low price. But despite the hotel boom of the twenties, household consumers accounted by far for the bulk of business, a purchasing trend that continued into the sixties when the reverse was more often the case.

By 1927, the industry's annual production of wool carpeting had reached 65,600,000 square yards, not its peak capacity—that had been reached in 1904 with a volume of 83,000,000 square yards. The major outside competitors were the makers of linoleum and of asphalt-base, hard-surface floorcoverings. Part of the loss of prestige was considered to be due to a strain from within the industry and a lack of concerted effort and intra-industry communication. To correct this, The Carpet Institute was incorporated as a non-profit organization in Delaware, with headquarters in Washington, D. C. The Institute's function was primarily

to act as clearing house for the collection and dissemination to members of information of value to the whole industry. The information was to be gathered both from within the industry, and from such outside sources as government agencies. It was to keep its members informed about legislation that might be significant, and it could see that the industry's views were presented promptly and effectively in appropriate legislative circles.

About the same time, interior decoration became something for the middle class—no longer limited to those of wealth, and aided by women's magazines edited by women, the average housewife became conscious of fashion in decoration and design. With the influx of highly styled furnishings from abroad, launched by the so-called "modern school" (through the Bauhaus), carpet companies found themselves faced with the need to add decorating departments. One of the first was Bigelow, which established a "home decorating bureau" to answer dealer inquiries on the many new designs and their proper settings. The trend from wall-to-wall or room-size rugs gave way to the brilliantly colored and patterned area rug with two-dimensional geometric areas of color. A mail-order business, through such concerns as Sears, Roebuck & Company and Montgomery Ward & Company, enabled carpet manufacturers to reach a new class of customer. Many manufacturers, noting the success of the mail-order business, began to develop their own catalogs. The patterns offered were not the regular stock but instead, smaller rugs woven specially for the purpose. Competition was heated, and by 1930 the mail-order business—their own or by outside agencies—absorbed much of the industry's production. As business boomed, the government changed the general tariff structure, which finally culminated in the Hawley-Smoot Tariff Act of 1930. American cotton growers wanted protection against imports of Indian jute, used in all carpet backings. And the search was on for substitutes for raw materials. Two new products made an interesting appearance. The first was a rayon-surfaced rug woven in combination with cotton. Cotton had barely been used in machine-made carpets before. But the use of rayon introduced the first man-made fiber to the industry. The rayon had a sheen which looked a little like silk, and when Bigelow produced its "Domestic Oriental," demand was so great that two mills could not keep up with it.

Carpet wool, the staple fiber for all rugs and carpets made in the United States, was beginning to vary in quality, coming as it did from many and sometimes remote parts of the world. Its price was subject to wide fluctuations, and mills taking advantage of a low market ran the risk of over-purchasing while underpurchasing during peak markets. By 1937 each mill was forced to find some other solution. Cotton seemed to be the only other natural fiber that could conceivably replace wool as a carpet fiber. But again, cotton prices fluctuated, particularly during a bad season and crop failures. Cotton also met with some consumer resistance.

Most companies turned to the man-made substitutes. Early rayon proved an unreliable fiber, not suited to the rugged demands made by carpets; it soiled easily, and it was not resilient. It was unstable when dyed. For a while it was believed that a part-wool, part-rayon carpet was the answer, but the public rejected that also. When the war was over, a new demand for carpets sorely taxed the industry's capacity. With the fluctuations of the available wool (its supply heavily curtailed by the Korean War) and rayon production insufficient, the industry turned to the synthetic fiber producers. The word synthetic had acquired a bad connotation during the war, but the manu-facturers felt that the resistance was due to the poor quality and not to the idea of synthetics *per se*. The proper use of synthetics could overcome this consumer resistance if a number of improvements could be made, and also by consumer education.

Fibers of the hydro-carbon type were investigated—Orlon, Saran, Chem-strand, Dynel and others—with some success. But it was not until the late fifties that the large synthetic producers, such as Dupont and Allied Chemical, gave the matter serious thought and began to work in tandem with the carpet manufacturer. The dual effort was to produce fibers that would weave attractively, take dye well, be more durable than wool, need less maintenance and have resiliency. By the late sixties, synthetics under a wide variety of trade names made up 85 per cent of the carpet industry's vast production. Wool became relegated to those luxury items still preferred by the interior designer for most homes.

Two other important factors helped to establish the healthy state in which the American carpet industry found itself during the late 1960's. The first was a gradual move during the thirties from the highly unionized and increasingly costly traditional manufacturing areas in New England and Pennsylvania, to more felicitous locations in the South. The advantages, as the carpet industry was to find out, were worth the prodigious effort, including as they did a large low-cost labor supply, easier accessibility to raw materials, the handling of these, and a better access to markets.

The first company to make the step was James Lees, which had risen to the position of one of the top four carpet producers by the later thirties. Lees found in 1938 a location in Glasgow, Virginia, and this bold step proved an interesting point: a company with traditional equipment could enhance its position within the market place by making this move to the South. By the early 1950's Lees became a serious challenger (in volume) to those reigning giants, Bigelow and Alexander Smith. With such precedence, it was natural that more carpet manufacturers would follow. During the 1950's the areas of North Georgia, South Carolina, and Virginia became dotted with large mills. In 1950 Bigelow purchased a small company, Georgian Rug Mill in Summerville, Georgia. This latest move precipitated not only another physical move on the part of one of the major northern manufacturers to the South, but it marked the first entry into the field of tufted goods (in this case cotton) by a manufacturer accustomed to woven carpets (mainly wool).

By the late sixties the marriage of synthetic fibers and the latest refinements of high speed, very narrow-gauge tufting machinery that could produce densely tufted goods in unlimited patterns set the industry booming. With the wide pricing structure possible by these methods, hardly a home within the United States did not have some kind of carpeting. Carpeting became specified (almost by the acre) for schools, hospitals, hotels, motels, and clubs.

With the majority of people within the country satisfied with a reasonably good quality product, chosen from a broad spectrum of colors and a wide range of plain, textured, or patterned carpets, something more was being demanded by those who preferred something exclusive, and by those interior designers who chose in many cases to design one-of-a-kind rugs or carpets for clients who pursued the expensive fashionable life. To satisfy that demand, a number of large carpet manufacturers set up small design studios within the main studios to handle this comparatively small segment of the business. Premium prices were charged for this custom service. Several small firms set up facilities for a service exclusive to the interior designer, manufacturing little or no mass-produced goods. During the early 20's a group of brothers from the Polish-American V'Soske family developed a hand-tufting method. Their original tools were primitive. Later they perfected a usable electric hand-tufting machine with interchangeable needles which could create a variety of textures prohibited by the power machine's limitations. Still later, a hand-carving tool, an outgrowth of sheep's shears, enabled the V'Soskes to carve an edging around tufted patterns, or to carve whole patterns within the main field of a rug. These important tools, according to the family's head designer, Stanislav V'Soske, "were able to release the designer from the restrictions necessarily imposed by the warp and weft of the traditional loom, and to offer versatility in the interpretation of design with a speed in manufacturing never before achieved in hand-made rugs." Original stock designs within the wholesale (trade) showrooms of both Edward Fields and V'Soske were generally created by "name" designers or were contemporized interpretations of traditional patterns. But all were subject to both color, scale, and even to pattern revisions to suit each individual client.

Many jobbers, importers, or dealers in showrooms, not having access to these small custom mills, "farmed" out their custom orders to existing mills either within the country or in other countries. The more favorite areas were Hong Kong, India, Portugal or Spain, where labor costs were decidedly cheaper, and where skilled weavers were trained to copy almost any pattern drawn and colored that was presented to them. This they could accomplish within a relatively short space of time. Other dealers imported Orientals (again very popular during the sixties), or antique Savonneries and Aubussons —always the favorite for the discriminate few.

American. Period bedroom, 1760–1770. *Nelson Fund. Collection of William Rockhill Nelson Gallery of Art, Atkins Museum of Fine Arts, Kansas City, Missouri.*

American, New England, 18th century (?). Hooked rug with leopard medallion and well designed asymmetrical border. Old Sturbridge Village photo. *Collection of Nina Fletcher Little.*

American, New England. Shirred rug on tow grain bag. 18th century (?). Old Sturbridge Village photo. *Collection of Nina Fletcher Little.*

American. Painted canvas floor cloth with geometric pattern. "Two Women" by Eunice Pinney 1770–1849. Watercolor c. 1810, Connecticut. *New York State Historical Collections.*

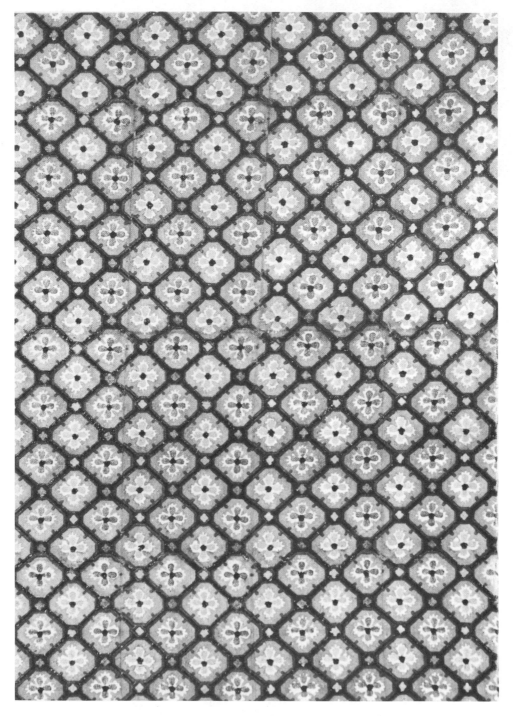

American, New England. 18th century (?). Floor cloth from Concord, New Hampshire. Old Sturbridge Village photo. *Collection of Nina Fletcher Little.*

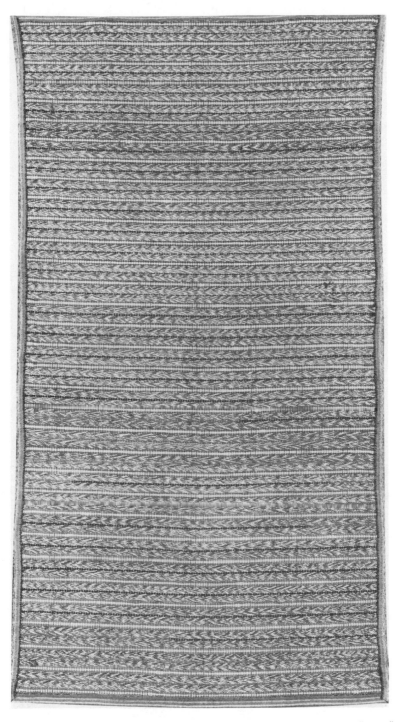

American. Shaker rug, tan, green, and blue wool. Size 56″ x 36″. *Given by Mr. and Mrs. Julius Zieget, Courtesy Philadelphia Museum of Art.*

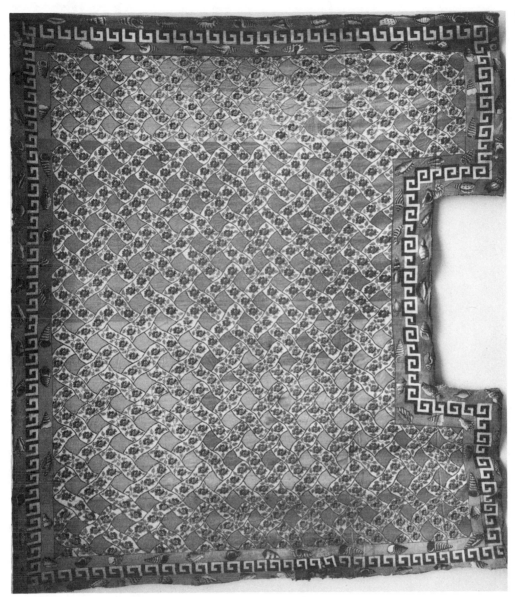

American, 1808–1812. Embroidered cross-stitch wool. From house of Judge Moore, Champlain, N. Y. Makers: Ann and Sophia Moore and Harriet Hicks, Champlain, N. Y. *The Metropolitan Museum of Art. Gift of Isabelle C. Mygatt, 1923.*

Opposite page, top: American. Drawing room, The Lindens, Danvers, Massachusetts, circa 1754. *Nelson Fund. Collection of William Rockhill Nelson Gallery of Art, Atkins Museum of Fine Arts, Kansas City, Missouri.*

Opposite, below: American. American wing. Haverhill Room. m8, Floor 1. September, 1946. *The Metropolitan Museum of Art.*

American, 1832–35. Zuzuah Higbey Guernsey embroidered her initials in script in a square at the top. She later became Mrs. Caswell. Embroidered in colored yarns and woolen fabrics. *The Metropolitan Museum of Art. Gift of Katherine Keyes, 1938. Memory of her father, Homer Eaton Keyes.*

American, circa 1825—New England. Applique rug on dark background. *The Metropolitan Museum of Art, Gift of Mrs. J. Insley Blair, 1942.*

American, early 19th century. Embroidered wool on wool. *Courtesy of The Art Institute of Chicago.*

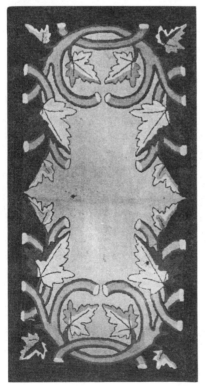

Opposite page:

Top: American, New England, 19th century. Hooked rug with unusual still life. Old Sturbridge Village photo. *Collection of Nina Fletcher Little.*

Below, left: American, early 19th century. Hooked rug. *Courtesy of The Art Institute of Chicago.*

Below, right: American, early 19th century. Hooked rug. *Courtesy of The Art Institute of Chicago.*

American, early 19th century (?). Hooked rug. *Courtesy of The Art Institute of Chicago.*

American, first half 19th century. Probably Vermont. Hooked rug with American eagle. The fourteen stars commemorate the admission of Vermont to the Union. *The Metropolitan Museum of Art. Rogers Fund, 1945.*

Left: American, early 19th century. Hooked rug. *Courtesy of The Art Institute of Chicago.*

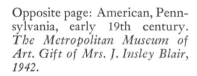

Opposite page: American, Pennsylvania, early 19th century. *The Metropolitan Museum of Art. Gift of Mrs. J. Insley Blair, 1942.*

Above: American, New England, early 19th century. Hooked rug. *The Metropolitan Museum of Art, Rogers Fund, 1918.*

Left: American, early 19th century. Hooked rug. *Courtesy of The Art Institute of Chicago.*

American, early 19th century. Hooked rug. *Courtesy of The Art Institute of Chicago.*

American, early 19th century. Hooked rug. *Courtesy of The Art Institute of Chicago.*

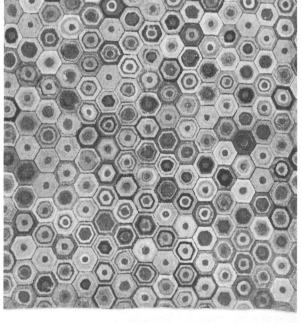

American, early 19th century. Hooked rug with "Star of Bethlehem" theorem. Two versions by two women. *Courtesy of The Art Institute of Chicago.*

Top: American, early 19th century. Hooked mat. *Courtesy of The Art Institute of Chicago.*

Above: American, mid-19th century. Hooked rug. *Courtesy of The Art Institute of Chicago.*

Right: American, late 19th century. Braided rug. *Courtesy of The Art Institute of Chicago.*

Opposite page: American, early 19th century. Hooked rug. *Courtesy of The Art Institute of Chicago.*

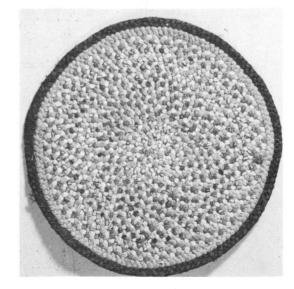

American. Hooked rug, polychrome. *The Metropolitan Museum of Art. Gift of Mr. George M. Moffett, 1936.*

Opposite page:

Top: American, late 19th century. Hooked rug. *Courtesy of The Art Institute of Chicago.*

Center: American, 19th century. Signed Lucy Bernard. "House with Horse in Foreground" on burlap yarn cloth. *The Metropolitan Museum of Art. Sansbury-Mills Fund, 1961.*

Bottom: American, 19th century. Lucy Bernard. House and Landscape within framework of trees and flowers of burlap, yarn, and cloth. *The Metropolitan Museum of Art. Sansbury-Mills Fund, 1961.*

American, 1870. Ingrain carpet (detail). *Courtesy of Bigelow-Sanford Company Museum.*

American, 1870. Brussels carpet (detail). From Lowell Manufacturing Company, one of the mills that merged to form present-day Bigelow-Sanford, Inc. *Courtesy Bigelow-Sanford Company Museum.*

Opposite page: American, 19th century. Hooked rug, wool on coarse canvas. *The Metropolitan Museum of Art. The Sylmaris Collection. Gift of George Coe Graus, 1930.*

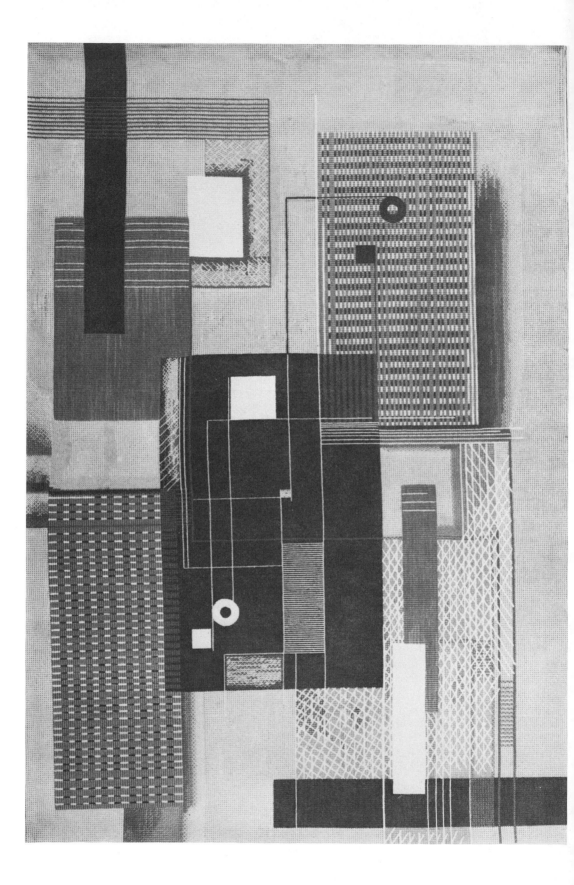

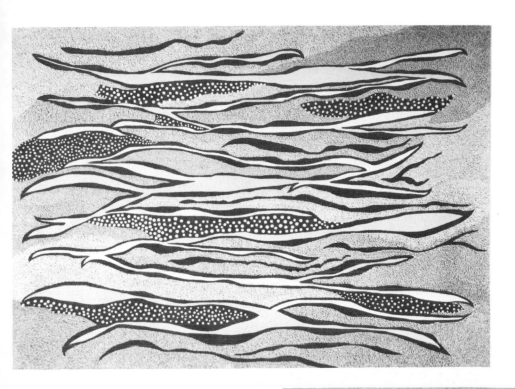

Opposite page: American, circa 1942. Designed by I. Rice Pereira. Abstract design with emphasis on textures in black, white, gray, and copper tones on gray. Executed by V'Soske for The Museum of Modern Art for the "New Rugs by American Artists" exhibition, 1942. *Courtesy The Museum of Modern Art.*

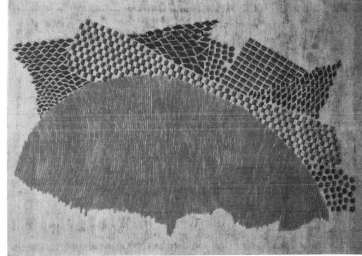

Top: American, 1959. "Grain," designed by Albert Herbert, executed by V'Soske. Stripe theme with interesting variations of broken or textured variations. *Courtesy V'Soske.*

Above: American, 1969. "Piza" (fragment of sun), designed by Arturo Luiz Piza of Brazil, executed by Stanislav V'Soske. Sophisticated use of many textured effects using worsted yarns. *Courtesy V'Soske.*

Left: American, early 1930's. Early hand-carved and brushed-wool pile modern rug. Carved by Bronyk V'Soske. *Courtesy V'Soske.*

214

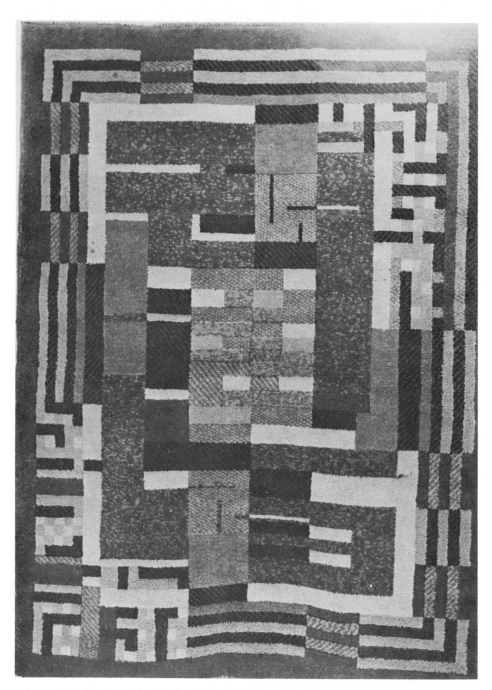

American, 1923. Designed by Benita Otte. A Weimer Bauhaus pattern, one of several which influenced American carpet design of the late 20's and early 30's. *Courtesy of Staatliche Kunstsammlungen, Weimer.*

American, 20th century, 1968. Tufted rug. "Short Circuit," a super charged design in red, magenta, orange, blue, and white. *Courtesy of Edward Fields*.

7 AMERICAN INDIAN

Too little recognition has been given to the crafts of the North American Indian, and considering that these crafts predate those of other ethnic groups in America, they are remarkably sophisticated. Not all Indian tribes produced textile weavers. Many preferred the nomadic life, roaming from one area of the country to the other in search of wild animals to hunt or running streams to fish. Other tribes cultivated other crafts, such as pottery or basket weaving. For textile weaving, some kind of fiber—wool or cotton—must be patiently cultivated, harvested, and painstakingly made into threads to prepare it for weaving.

Cotton was the first fiber harvested in the United States. It was grown in the Southwest by the Pueblo Indians of New Mexico. From it these people wove fabrics apparently of such fineness and beauty that the Spaniards (after their conquest of Mexico and nearby territories in the sixteenth century) put great value on the cloth. (Archeologists believe that the Pueblo men had been perfecting their skill from 700 A.D.) A tax was imposed upon the Pueblo in the form of woven cloth, with each family assessed a tribute of 33 inches (one *varo*) of finished material annually. In turn, the cloth was sent to headquarters in Mexico, then to Spain. But as pressures by the Spanish 219 on the Pueblo increased, leading finally to the Pueblo Rebellion of 1680, the Indians moved to avoid reprisals. Many went north to join a fellow group, the Navajos. The few that remained virtually gave up the craft of weaving, preferring instead to use European cloths and clothes, saving their native dress for ceremonial occasions.

The Navajos who aided their fellow Pueblos were not craft oriented. Instead they were a restless nomadic group, preferring in those days to hunt the open ranges and to maraud the Spanish as well as other tribal outposts. They did raise sheep, the flocks multiplying from those few sheep originally stolen from the Spanish. (The early army of Coronado had brought almost 5,000 sheep with them when they had set out from Spain in "conquest of the Seven Cities of Cibola"—an unfulfilled dream.) The sheep were a particularly hardy breed called Churro, raised mainly by Spanish peasants. And although they appeared scrawny and spindly-legged, they did possess a fleece whose staples were long and straight, making them easy to spin and weave. When the Pueblos moved north, they brought with them pods from their cotton to plant in the new territory. And by 1700, in the natural course of events, (having an abundant supply of both cotton and wool fibers plus skilled teachers available), the Navajo women had learned to weave. The question has arisen whether their teachers possibly were the Spaniards, but it is an indisputable fact that the primitive weaving methods adopted by the Navajo were certainly not Spanish. As Navajo women perfected their craft, the Pueblo men forgot it, and today among the Pueblo tribes only an occasional belt is woven for the tourist.

The Classic Period—1850–1875
The Period of the First Weavers

Fragments of the earliest Navajo blankets, the forerunners of rugs, appear to have been unadorned or bore only primitive striped patterns, apparently adapted from an earlier Pueblo style. In fact, there seems to be little or no variation in the stripe prior to 1850. As expertise grew, quality became decidedly refined, eventually superseding that of the Pueblo teachers. Among the few samples woven prior to 1850 which still exist, the sophisticated tapestry weave seems to have been common.

The most popular colors, other than those natural wool colors, were indigo blue and, later, a red. Indigo was purchased from the Spaniards and came in the form of large chunks from Mexico. Within the pattern yarns dyed with this blue were carefully balanced against natural black (a brownish color), white, or gray. When greenish tints highlighted the darker colors, it was an indication that those colors had been deepened in tone by some vegetable dye. For the red, the Indians obtained a red woolen material from the Spaniards, (by way of Mexico) which they unraveled, weaving the threads into the blanket. These blankets became known as bayeta blankets, a word taken from *bayeto* or *vayeta*, Spanish words for "baize." The bayeta was a type of cloth originally woven in Spain, later woven in England for export to Spain and eventually to Mexico, where it was sold to the Indians for a fixed price of six dollars a pound. Bayeta wool was used occasionally in the so-called chief's blanket or ceremonial robes.

The Navajo had her own method for carding and spinning. No implement has ever been found, and the conclusion has been that the process was done by hand, chiefly by rolling fibers between the palm of the hand and the bare thigh or calf of the leg. But wool with any curl to it at all would have been most difficult to spin into threads by this method. Therefore, it has been surmised that some weavers must have used some sort of rudimentary appliance to help in the spinning process.

The Navajo looms were of the simplest type possible—an upper and a lower beam on which the warp was stretched and tied. This contraption was generally tied to the branch of a tree to make it more accessible to the woman who sat on the ground. Narrow sticks were threaded through the warp threads to keep sheds in place. As a beater, the weaver used a flat, smooth piece of wood to push the rows of colored weft wools tightly into the growing fabric.

During this early period the Navajos wove blankets, sometimes called "dougies" (which tourists and collectors have often used as rugs) and saddle blankets, but few actual rugs (they did not use them). The most elaborate were the chief's blankets, which in time became prized objects in trade with tribes whose women did not or could not weave. A few of the blankets were double woven, an extremely intricate process resulting in a different pattern on each side, usually striped on one and some other geometry on the other. The skill of the weaving appeared in the evenness of the surface.

Prior to 1850 the basic colors of these chief's blankets appeared to have been the natural wool colors of black and white woven into stripes. Later, chief's blankets had corner designs and a central rectangular motif. The top, bottom and center bands were in indigo and the corners and rectangles of bayeta red. For variation, the striped pattern leaned heavily on simple, straight-edged geometrics such as narrow rectangles, crosses, zig-zags, or diamond shapes. These often produced steps or "terraces" running in diagonals.

Of those blankets made for the Navajo's own use, many had "terrace" patterns worked into a solid color ground. Others had finely tailored stripes behind the general pattern. Occasionally, these were broken with short parallel bars, or the central stripe was enlarged and the corners marked by diagonal stripes or solid color triangles.

The years 1863 to 1868 were dark years for the Navajo. As punishment for their constant plundering of other tribes and of Spanish territories, they were rounded up by Kit Carson and impounded in a forty acre reservation, the Bosque Redondo, at Fort Sumner in east central New Mexico. Textile weaving barely survived this tragedy, for the Indians were issued commercially made cloth—velveteen for the women and bleached muslin for the men for their trousers, pleasing to them at the time.

The Transition Period—1875–1890

The early fibers, handspun wool dyed with indigo, or bayeta, and Saxony yarns disappeared during this period. Instead, threads were unraveled from commercial fabrics and used. Later, coarse handspun threads dyed with aniline dyes or wools from Germantown, Pennsylvania, replaced those unraveled threads. But in both cases the colors were harsh, unattractive, and inclined to run. Cotton twine was used for warps, replacing wool or Saxony. Patterns changed. Small diamond or triangular patterns emerged, showing a more sophisticated attitude toward weaving. It was during this period that small animals, figures, or other pictorial ideas such as trains, or whatever form caught the weaver's imagination at the time, were used in both rugs and blankets. The figures seemed stylized or somewhat angular—a result of the technical limitations of the weave itself.

In spite of a popularly held belief, it is now concluded by anthropologists and students of Indian mores, that most of the symbols or figures woven into rugs and blankets were in no way ritualistic. They were purely decorative elements, woven mainly to attract the tourist's eye. This includes those divinity figures, "Yeis," which appear in so-called "sand painting" patterns or used in multiples in what is called the Yeibichai rug. The fact is that when "Yei" rugs were first noticed by the tribal elders in the Farmington and Lukachukai Mountain areas about 1900, there was much opposition to using any kind of divinity figure for commercial use. But as rugs were never used for ceremonial use, the objections were eventually withdrawn.

The railroad was pushing further west, finally reaching New Mexico and Arizona about the end of the century, opening up those areas to tourists and bringing in a flow of commercially made products, in particular, textiles. In time these textiles did away with the necessity of weaving blankets for home use. And once again, the craft would have met with extinction if it had not been for the tourist, who realized the beauty and picturesque charm of Indian blankets (which could be used as rugs) and who was anxious to purchase.

The Rug Period—1890–1920

Officially, the weaving of rugs as such began in 1890, and in spite of traders who tried to maintain some standard of quality, the early rugs (until 1920) were inferior to the old blankets. Many were "gaudy," made with wools dyed with poor commercial dyes in a range of colors the Indians had not seen before. In fact, the Indian weavers at first were inclined to go "wild" with color, showing no concern for the balance of color within the pattern and definitely lacking their earlier sensitivity in the selection of a subtle palette.

The wool they were using was from merino sheep, a recent acquisition brought into the reservation in order to strengthen the herds. Merino wool is greasy and unless meticulously washed does not take dye well. Traders anxious to sell as many rugs as possible became more interested in quantity rather than demanding quality, purchasing as many as possible by the pound. Rugs with greasy wool weighed more than clean wool rugs, and to make them even heavier a number of Indians resorted to pounding sand into the wool. (Interestingly enough, although new materials and new dyes were being used, the ancient method of weaving remained the same.) To attract attention, some Navajo weavers would cart looms out to the crossroads, often being driven to the spot. There they would sit and weave all day, being picked up in the evening, only to return the next clear day.

Contemporary Navajo Rugs

The consistent development of Navajo rug weaving in the past years is characterized by a remarkably subtle palette plus a refinement of the basic tapestry weave. In many cases the Navajo weaver has returned to many of the earlier vegetable dyes and the use of natural wools for their rugs—a welcome sophistication. The brightly colored rug has come a long way from those inferior and garish rugs of the "Transitional Period" and "Early Rug Period." This present and happier state of affairs is largely due to the efforts of the United States Government which, in 1935, set up a cooperative research agency, the South Western Range and Sheep Breeding Laboratory at Fort Wingate, New Mexico. The object was to improve the quality of both wool and meat. Over the years there had been an indiscriminate breeding of the sheep that roamed the plains and mesas around the Navajo reservation, which had in time weakened the herds. The wool produced from the government-bred sheep was ideal for weaving, having a low percentage of crimp or curl, and was almost greaseless. The laboratory also developed a training program for shearing the sheep in an effort to improve the quality or length of staple to make it easier to spin. The new and better wools, curiously enough, inspired the Navajos into producing a finer product.

During the thirties dyes and dye methods were also improved, largely due to the efforts of one Navajo, Mrs. Nonabah G. Bryan, who was at that time employed at the Fort Wingate Vocational High School operated by the Bureau of Indian Affairs, U.S. Department of Interior. Mrs. Bryan, exploiting the vast resources of the reservation, developed over eighty natural vegetable-dye recipes which were published in 1940. One recipe appears in Gilbert Maxwell's informative booklet, *Navajo Rugs*.

. . . from the cliff rose, a dye that turns wool a golden hue. Two pounds of fresh cliff rose twigs, and leaves; ¼ cup raw alum; one pound of yarn. Boil the twigs and leaves in five gallons of water for two hours. Strain. Add raw alum to dye-water. Stir and let boil ten minutes. Add the wet yarn and stir again. Boil for two hours. Allow to remain in the dye bath overnight. Rinse.

The recipes in Mrs. Bryan's booklet give directions for eighty-four lovely pastel colors or shades.

Her efforts have been reflected in many beautiful, subtle monotone rugs we see today, in particular those from the Chinle, Wide Ruins, and Nazlini territories.

Largely responsible for the growth of the Navajo rug industry and the quality to which the weavers adhere are the various traders who have controlled the thirteen major trading areas scattered around the vast Navajo reservations. These men, dedicated to the Indian and to his crafts, have monitored the quality and output of contemporary rugs. In some cases, as in Shiprock-Red Rocks (named for a giant volcanic formation called Shiprock) the Yei blanket or rug was developed commercially by the trader-owner of the Shiprock Trading Company, Will Evans.

Today the thirteen trading areas, each having its own distinctive and dynamic style, are producing for the collector rugs of the finest quality which can no longer be considered solely for the tourist. Instead, these have been woven for those who appreciate sophisticated designs, subtly colored, in fine weaves and weights, and rugs from some territories command prices which can range up to several thousand dollars.

The main characteristics of those rugs from the trading post at Wide Ruins are the vegetal dyes used—black from pinon pitch, sumac, or ochre; red from the root of the mountain mahogany (this is unusual, for most reds have been bayeta cloth red, or made from an aniline dye); and an occasional touch of yellow made from the rabbit's bush. Largely responsible for the refinements of color and weave at this post are the husband and wife team, the Lippincotts, who purchased the trading post in 1938. They demanded, and received, only those rugs which adhered to their high standard. Because of the delicacy of the colors, designs in this area are understandably simple, usually bearing vertical stripes, or stripes combined with large central rectangles or diamonds creating terrace patterns. Somewhat similar are those rugs from the Naziline or Chinle area located at Canyon de Chelley (Chinle means "at the mouth of the canyon"), where vegetal-dye rugs are also woven. An additional khaki color is found here. Stripes within these simple borderless patterns appear to be serrated edges. "Yei" rugs woven with vegetal-dye yarns are also found here. These have small, generally attenuated or stylized divinity figures taken from old sand paintings, quite amusingly "framed" on three sides with the elongated rainbow figure. More colorful Yei rugs come from the Shiprock territory, where they have been known to be woven with as many as fifteen different colors against a white background.

The figures of these Yei rugs differ somewhat from those Yeibichai figures (Navajos impersonating the Yei figure) and are also found at Shiprock. The latter are used in multiples and the rugs are considerably large in size.

Near Washington Pass is the trading post, Crystal Rocks, where J. B. Moore was director for a number of years. Because this post was, and still is, closed in winter, Moore created a mail-order catalog for an eastern clientele. Moore has also been accredited with redesigning the rug patterns found in that territory, making them more "Indian"—something he felt was needed to attract customers who had never before seen an Indian rug. His patterns somewhat resembled beadwork designs and were in bright colors. Much red was evident. This was back in 1911. Since then the weavers of Crystal Rock have reverted to indigenous patterns woven with delicately colored vegetal-dye yarns. Today's Crystal rugs are recognizable by their stripes, many bearing small geometric designs within the wider stripes.

Probably the finest of all rugs come from the Two Gray Hills area. These are distinguished by their symmetry of geometric forms, not unlike that of the Oriental rug from the Middle East. The colors are natural white, black, gray, and brown. Gray was created by spinning fine threads of black and white together. Similar in their geometric designs are those rugs from the Tees pos nos trading post in northeastern Arizona. These are more colorful, having been woven of yarns dyed with a superior type aniline dye, or on occasion, woven with a fine quality commercial yarn. The Tees pos nos rug is not, in spite of the brighter colors, quite as dramatic as those from Two Gray Hills, due mainly to the diffusion of the many major geometric forms within one pattern.

Another forceful and dynamic rug comes from the Ganado Area. Perhaps these best express today what an Indian rug should look like. These are woven with a lustrous, glowing aniline-dyed yarn (possibly dyed double strength) known as Ganado red. The colors fill in large diamond or other geometric forms which are outlined in black. As weavers in this area have recently become influenced by the soft colorations obtained by vegetal dyes, the color red is diminishing.

One of the most interesting, if not the most popular, patterns is found in the "storm pattern" rug woven around Tuba City, (but found in any number of other territories). The name is a misnomer, for like the Yei rug there is no mystical or religious meaning to the design. Instead, the name was attached to the design by J. B. Moore of Crystal Springs, New Mexico while compiling his catalog of Indian rug designs in 1911. The design in question bears a central square block of color (variously called the hogan, or storm house); radiating from this central block are zig-zag lines (lightning?) which end in four corner blocks of color. Within those blocks are small, insect-like figures identified as "water bugs," or "pinyon beetles." Regardless of the authenticity of the design, these "storm pattern" rugs are truly Indian in origin.

Nearby is the trading post of Coal Mine Mesa which during the early sixties was an experimental station for the improvement of the quality of weave within the the area. The project was under the direction of a Navajo, Ned Hatathli, former manager of the Navajo Arts and Crafts Guild, who apparently financed the effort from his own pocket. The project was highly successful, for today Navajo women are weaving the finest double-weave—a highly complicated weave—rugs found on the reservation. These are usually grays and white, or natural.

Although we have categorically listed many of the styles and colors of rugs found within the Navajo reservation, we must hasten to add that all of the styles mentioned, as well as those not mentioned, have been found in many territories or trading centers other than their "home" trading post. As women travel about the reservation in their own cars, or as marriages move young female weavers to some other territory, designs and colors move with them. Bored with repetition, many Navajo weavers improvise on the same theme by bringing into them ideas found in other areas. For few of the rugs found anywhere were designed by artists or "name" designers. Instead, as we have already pointed out, the designs evolved over a number of years, sometimes guided by the owner or manager of a trading post seeking an individual style. But these were almost always refinements on an indigenous style already found somewhere within the area.

American Indian. Navajo, Arizona. Double weave, saddle blanket, 29″ wide. *Courtesy of Museum of the American Indian. Heye Foundation.*

American Indian. Navajo women weaving and spinning in front of hogan. *Courtesy of Museum of New Mexico.*

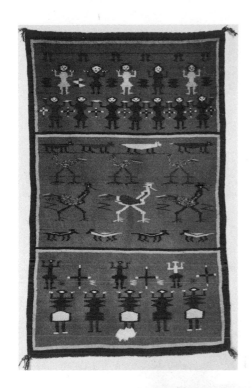

American Indian, circa 1890, Navajo, New Mexico. Woven blanket of Germantown yarn. Small multi-colored human and animal figures (road runners) woven on red background. *Courtesy of Museum of the American Indian. Heye Foundation.*

American Indian, 1880–1890. Navajo. Very large blanket of blue, black and white stripes and frets. Collected by Colonel J. T. Clarke. *Courtesy of Museum of the American Indian. Heye Foundation.*

American Indian, Navajo, New Mexico. Wool blanket of Germantown yarn. *Courtesy of Museum of the American Indian. Heye Foundation.*

American Indian, Navajo, New Mexico. Blanket of Germantown yarn. *Courtesy of Museum of the American Indian. Heye Foundation.*

American Indian, Navajo, New Mexico.
Chief's blanket. *Courtesy of the American Indian Museum. Heye Foundation.*

American Indian, Navajo, New Mexico.
Wool blanket. *Courtesy of Museum of
the American Indian. Heye Foundation.*

American Indian, Navajo. Yeibichai blanket in the possession of Mrs. Thea Heye. *Courtesy of Museum of the American Indian. Heye Foundation.*

American Indian, Navajo, New Mexico. Wool blanket. *Courtesy of the American Indian Museum. Heye Foundation.*

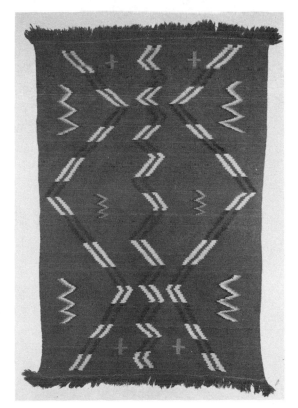

234

American Indian, Navajo, New Mexico. Germantown wool. Includes small human figures. *Courtesy of Museum of the American Indian. Heye Foundation.*

American Indian, Navajo, New Mexico. Blanket. *Courtesy of Museum of the American Indian. Heye Foundation.*

American Indian, Navajo, New Mexico. Blanket. *Courtesy of Museum of the American Indian. Heye Foundation.*

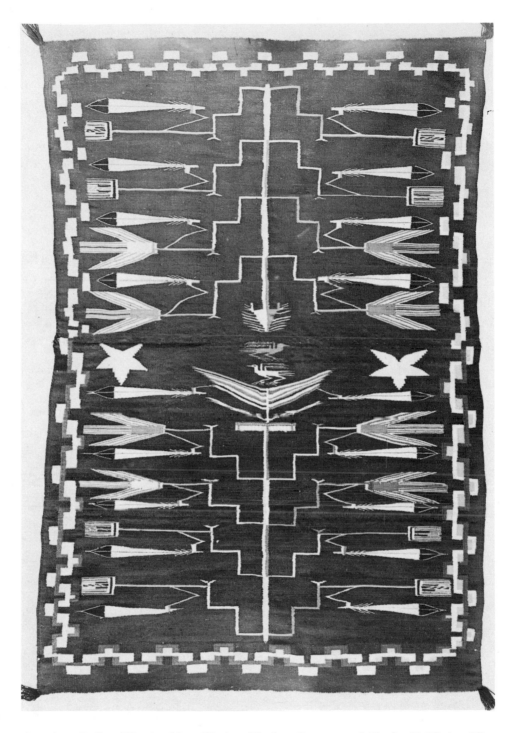

American Indian, Navajo, New Mexico. Blanket. Property of Charles F. Nesler, New-ark, New Jersey. *Courtesy of Museum of the American Indian. Heye Foundation.*

American Indian, Navajo, Arizona. Six Yeibichai figures. *Courtesy of Museum of the American Indian. Heye Foundation.*

American Indian, Navajo, New Mexico. Yei figure. Sandpainting figure. *Courtesy of the Museum of the American Indian. Heye Foundation.*

American Indian, Navajo, New Mexico. Wool
blanket, purchased 1900, with white background
and figures of horses, bows and arrows. *Courtesy
of Museum of the American Indian. Heye Foundation.*

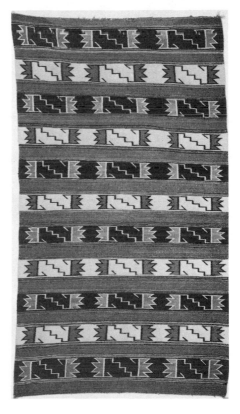

American Indian, Navajo, New Mexico. Crystal.
Banded design in red, blue and gray. *Courtesy of
Museum of the American Indian. Heye Founda-
tion.*

American Indian, Navajo, New Mexico. Germantown yarns. *Courtesy of Museum of the American Indian. Heye Foundation.*

American Indian, Navajo, 1951. Two Gray Hills type. Created by Daisy Taugle Chee. *Collection of William Rockhill Nelson Gallery of Art, Atkins Museum of Fine Arts, Kansas City, Missouri.*

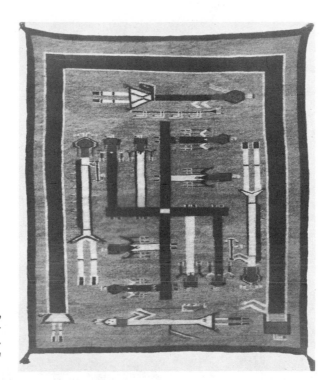

American Indian, Navajo, 1930. Whirling logs rug, similar to some sand paintings. *Courtesy of Museum of New Mexico.*

American Indian, Navajo. Chief's blanket (early). *Courtesy of Museum of New Mexico.*

American Indian. Hope blanket. Lightning pattern. *Courtesy Museum of New Mexico.*

American Indian, Navajo. Yei rug with six figures, three on each side. *Courtesy Museum of New Mexico.*

American Indian, Navajo. Picture rug, with two horses and Indians at bottom, and stylized figures, arrows, birds and animals. *Courtesy Museum of New Mexico.*

American Indian, Navajo. Picture rug with trains, animals, birds and people. *Courtesy of Museum of New Mexico.*

American Indian. Navajo woman weaving double weave rug. Gallup Ceremonial, 1948. *Courtesy Museum of New Mexico.*

BIBLIOGRAPHY

Broadlooms and Businessmen: Ewing, John S. and Norton, Nancy P. Harvard Business Press, Cambridge, 1955.

Catalog of Spanish Rugs, 12th century to 19th century: Kühnel, Ernest and Bellinger, Louise. National Publishing Company, Washington, D.C., 1953.

Ciba Review: Volume 2 #20. April, 1939.

Elements of Interior Design and Decoration: Whiton, Sherrill. J. B. Lippincott Company, New York, 1951.

Fine Carpets in the Victoria and Albert Museum: with an introduction and descriptive notes by Kendrick, A. F. and Tattersall, C. E. C. Ernest Benn Ltd., London, 1924.

Flamskvavnader I Skäne: Fischer, Ernest. Bokforlaget Corona AB, Lund, Sweden, 1962.

Floorcoverings in 18th Century America: Roth, Rodris. Smithsonian Press, Washington, D.C., 1967.

Great Interiors, Edited by Grant, Ian: Preface by Beaton, Cecil. George Weidenfall and Nicholson Ltd., London; E. P. Dutton & Company, Inc., New York, 1967.

Greek Island Embroidery: Johnstone, Pauline. Alec Tiranti Ltd., London, 1961.

Handweaver and Craftsman: Volume 18, Number 2, Spring, 1967. Handweaver and Craftsman, Inc. Lancaster, Penna.

Handwoven Carpets, Oriental and European: Volume 1, Kendrick and Tattersall; Ben Brothers Ltd., London, 1922.

Les Châteaux de l'Ile de France, Collections Réalités: Preface by d'Ormesson, Wladimir Librairie Hachette et Société d'Etudes et de Publications Economiques, 1963.

Les Styles Francais, La Decoration du Moyen Âge au Modern Style: Editions Plaisirs de France, Paris, 1965.

Les Tapis d'Orient: Hangelblian, Armen E. Guy le Prat, Editor, Paris (no date given).

243

Mon Ami le Coq de Lurçat: Milhaud, Jean. Nouvelles Editions Latines, Paris, 1961.

Navajo Rugs . . . Past . . . Present and Future: Maxwell, Gilbert. Desert Southwest, Inc., Palm Desert, California, 1963.

Navajo Weaving, Its Techniques and Its History: Amsden, Charles Avery. The Fine Arts Press, Santa Ana, California, 1934.

Nouveau Larousse Universal: Librarie Larousse, Paris, 1948.

Spanish Copies of Turkish Carpets: Erdmann, Kurt and Hanna. Pantheon IV, Nov./Dec., 1965, Bruckmann Munches.

Suomen Ryijyt, Tak Stiilihistoriallinen Tutkimus: Sirelius, U. T. Kustannusosakeyhtio Otava, 1924 (limited and signed editions only).

Tapestries and Carpets from the Palace of the Prado (exhibition catalog Corcoran): G. P. Putnam, New York, 1917.

Textile Museum Journal: Volume 1, Number 1. Graphics Arts Press, Inc., Washington, D.C., November, 1962.

The Book of Rugs Oriental and European: Schlosser, Ignaz. Bonanza Books, New York, div. Crown Publishing, Inc., 1963.

The Connoisseur Period Guides: The Tudor Period, The Stuart Period, The Early Georgian Period, The Late Georgian Period, The Regency Period, The Early Victorian Period. Reynal & Company, New York, 1958.

The Charles Deering Collection, Carpets of Spain and the Orient: Berberyan, Stepan and Thomson, W. G. Private publication, no date given (limited edition).

The Flatwoven Kilims of the East: Ellis, Charles Grant. Textile Museum paper, Washington, D.C.

The Folk Arts and Crafts of New England: Lord, Priscilla Sawyer and Foley, Daniel J. Chilton Book Company, Philadelphia, 1965.

The Handwoven Fabrics of Thessaly: National Organization of Hellenic Handicrafts, Athens, 1961.

The Mirror of History (a supplement): Janson, H. W. Time Life Library of Art, Time, Inc., New York.

The Presence of Spain: Morris, James and Hofer, Evelyn. Harcourt, Brace and World, New York, 1964.

The Story of British Carpets: Jacobs, Bertrand. British Continental Trade Press Ltd., London, 1968.

The Story of Navajo Weaving: Kent, Kate Peck. The Heard Museum of Anthropology and Primitive Arts, Phoenix, Arizona, 1961.

The Textile Arts: Birrell, Verla. Harper & Brothers, New York, 1959.

The Tradition of French Fabrics: Brunschwig, Zelina.

Works in Architecture of R. and J. Adam, a Biographical Tribute: Swarbriek, John Quadrangle Books, Chicago, 1959.

INDEX

Jeanne G. Weeks, a native of Georgia, was educated in North Carolina, and has lived the major part of her professional life in New York. She was formerly on the staff of *American Home Magazine* and for the past several years she has been on the staff of *Interiors*, first as roving editor, and presently managing editor. She is married to Robert Oppenheimer, a native of France, and when not writing and living in New York, they make their home in Switzerland for several weeks each year.

Donald Treganowan is considered the "carpet-man's carpet man" in the industry. Mr. Treganowan learned all about carpets from his father who founded the firm, Ernest Treganowan, Inc., back in 1917. The romance of hand-made carpets soon appealed most to him. He has devoted most of his energies to the search for the unusual in "romance underfoot." His interest has taken him to almost every part of the world where fine carpets are made. His search for the unique hand-made carpets is more than just business, says Mr. Treganowan. "It is the passing on a thing of lasting beauty, an art from that reflects the society and culture where it is made." Mr. Treganowan is Vice President of the firm founded by his father and continues to search the world for "romance underfoot."